BEFORE LEAVING THIS EARTH, KNOW YOUR PMA:

Purpose, Mission, and Assignment

Before Leaving This Earth, Know Your PMA:

Purpose, Mission, and Assignment

Dorothy R. Swygert

Before Leaving this Earth, Know Your PMA: Purpose, Mission, and Assignment

Printed in the United States of America

ISBN: 978-0-9912306-2-4

Library of Congress Control Number: 2016952668

Published by:

Rekindle the Heart
Post Office Box 219
Hampton, VA 23669

*This book is dedicated to God
and
humanity.*

Contents

FOREWORD

I met Dorothy R. Swygert through a mutual friend almost twenty years ago. It was a fortuitous meeting. Through her books Dr. Swygert sounds the alarm on the ills threatening to destroy our society and country. Her books, Healing the Nation: *An In-Depth Study of African-Americans* and *Silence in a Democracy: Prisons for Profit: 21ˢᵗ Century Modern-day Slavery* are a wake-up call. Her carefully researched book *Silence in a Democracy: Prisons for Profit* details statistics on the alarming rates of incarceration of African American males in the United States of America.

If *Healing the Nation* and *Silence in a Democracy: Prisons for Profit* are wake-up calls, then her new book, *Before Leaving this Earth, Know Your PMA: Purpose, Mission, and Assignment* is a CALL TO ACTION! It is the voice of "one crying in the wilderness," calling us to return to our spiritual, Christ-centered roots. It reminds us of our national identity. Dr. Swygert has chosen ten extraordinary persons who knew their purpose, accepted their missions, and acted on their assignments. Through the mini-biographies of ten visionary people who used their gifts and talents to change the world, Dr. Dorothy R. Swygert has shown us how to put faith into action!

We are living in a time when many of us are being led astray. We are falling prey to the many ills in our society. There is a disintegration of family and community life, a continual assault on the public school system, and a falling away from the deep, abiding spiritual faith and values that have guided us throughout our history in this country. Dr. Dorothy R. Swygert has, in her new book, shown us how to find our way back. You will be the better for sharing this book with the youth of this generation.

Sarah Locke
Educator and Creative Artist

PREFACE

In *Before Leaving this Earth, Know Your PMA,* you will learn how Thaddaeus Stevens, born with a clubfoot, experienced taunts from classmates, was left brokenhearted by his father's desertion, and was nurtured by his mother to be all he could be. You will learn how he pulled himself up to become a lawyer and used his professional skills to fight for laws to make education in Pennsylvania free for all children. These pages will also describe how Stevens climbed the ladder to be seated in 1849 in the U.S. House of Representatives, where he fought vehemently to eradicate slavery from the nation and to make America truly the "land of the free and the home of the brave."

You will glimpse the soul of Dorothea Dix (1802-1887), who made it her life's mission to advocate for the rights of and services for the mentally-ill population. During her visits, she found horrible living conditions: "prisoners flogged, starved, chained, physically and sexually abused by their keepers, and left naked and without heat or sanitation." She had a soul conviction when she viewed such horrific conditions and began her asylum movement. She spent forty years of her life lobbying United States and Canadian legislators to establish state hospitals for the mentally ill. Because of her conviction, she devoted her energies to this cause, and her work led to the building of thirty-two institutions in the United States [history.com].

You will smile all the way back to the 1770s when you realize Abigail Adams was, in spirit, a woman of the twenty-first century. She was educated in her father's library, and her husband, John Adams, the second president of the United States, encouraged her to contribute as his equal to the writing of laws for our nation as it was being formed. Martin Luther King, Jr. of the twentieth century would have embraced her as his sister as she challenged the colonies with a profound truth when she said, "It always appeared a most iniquitous scheme to me to fight ourselves for what we are daily robbing and plundering from those who have as much a right to freedom as we have." While keeping her husband inspired, she managed a farm in Massachusetts, maintained a household, and cared for their children.

You will whisper secret prayers for Harriet Tubman when you read how she suffered a traumatic head wound when an irate slave master hit her with a heavy iron weight which was intended for another slave. She hovered between life and death while her parents used herbal medicines and prayers to restore her health. You will smile in delight when she arrives in Philadelphia as a free woman, and your heart will palpitate with joy to learn how she made it her life's mission to guide hundreds of other slaves to freedom as the conductor of her Underground Railroad.

You will sympathize with John the Baptist as you hear his daily message in the Jordan River: "Repent, for the kingdom of God is at hand," but you will cry when you learn he was decapitated at King Herod's command.

You will travel to Europe with Charles Sumner and see his transformative ideas come alive when he observes blacks and whites working together to study and do research. You will watch as he experiences a revelation: "Learning is not based on race and color." (At that time, in the late 1830s, blacks were prohibited from receiving an education.) You will feel his passion as he returns to the United States to become a senator and work vehemently to abolish slavery. But you will feel his pain and suffering when a fellow congressman attacks and beats him within an inch of his life with a gutta-percha gold-head cane on May 22, 1856. Rep. Preston Brooks of South Carolina carried out the attack because of a speech Sumner had made against the spread of slavery across the nation.

You will walk with twelve-year-old Booker T. Washington in 1865 as he travels from Virginia on the road to freedom with his mother, sister, and brother to arrive in West Virginia to work in the salt and coal mines. You will feel his deep, heartfelt yearning for an education. Your ears, like his, will perk up when you hear some old men talk about a school for blacks located in Hampton, Virginia, but you will experience along with him the difficulties of travel: trying to catch a ride, scrapping for a meal, and sleeping underneath steps until finally arriving in a disheveled state at Hampton Institute. There, the admission counselor gives him an admissions test, asking him to clean a room, chairs, and desks. You will shout for joy when he graduates from college in 1875. You will cry when he is sent by principal Samuel Armstrong to serve as principal at a school in Alabama, only to find his destination is an old Methodist church with a leaky roof. But you will cheer him on as he rolls up his sleeves and builds from scratch Tuskegee Institute, finding his life's mission.

Travel the night road of 1865 in post-Civil-War Missouri to witness night riders snatch an ex-slave, her daughter, and her baby boy from a farm and ride off into the night looking to make a sale. Hired by farm owner Moses Carver to bring them back, an ex-Civil War soldier found only the baby, who was discovered under a tree, sickly and almost dead. Susan Carver nursed the baby back to health, but young George was always frail.

Having compassion for his delicate nature, she refused to let him work in the fields. Instead, she taught him domestic work. After completing these chores, he had plenty of time to romp in the forest and grow in wisdom there, acquiring knowledge about the plants and flowers.

Follow the growth and development of George W. Carver as he seeks educational opportunities during the post-Civil-War years. He faced challenges, but he persevered until he became the first black to graduate from Iowa State College in 1894. He received his graduate degree in 1896 and was invited to join the faculty. Feel the compassionate spirit of Booker T. Washington as displayed in his letter to George Washington Carver, in which he begs the scientist to come help him educate the former slaves. Upon Carver's arrival in Tuskegee, you will cry when you learn there was no science department and he had to search the dump to find the supplies to build one.

You will applaud James V. Bennett as he completes his tour of duty in World War I, enrolls in law school, and is offered employment in the prison system. He read many books about prisons, but when he took a tour, the sights were so atrocious that he became nauseous and could not complete the visit. Upon returning home to his wife, he said, "I cannot work in the prisons." When he told his wife, "I don't know why I should be my brother's keeper," her answer was a question: "Why *not* be your brother's keeper?" Bennett accepted the employment, and within a year he had written a manual for the rehabilitation of prisoners. He found his mission and worked in the prisons, innovating laws and programs, until his retirement in 1964.

You will bow in reverence when you read about the death of Jesus, as he shed his blood on the cross for redemption of humanity, and spoke his last words: "Father, forgive them; for they know not what they do" (Luke 23:34).

Through all the tears and laughter, you will be inspired to assess your own life to identify your own purpose, mission, and assignment. Engage now in the mini biographies of ten superstars, each of whom embraced their purpose, mission, and assignment before leaving this earth.

ACKNOWLEDGMENTS

Consulting with other practitioners in the field of child-rearing has been most helpful in writing this book. I am grateful to Omar Swygert for reading this manuscript and applying his skills with editing the Youth Section.

I would like to extend my appreciation to Dr. Samori Swygert, who took time to read the manuscript and to give valuable assistance in recommending chapter coordination to provide continuity in this work.

I thank Sarah Locke for reading the manuscript and providing alternative narratives to address current crises confronting young adults.

Bernice Hendricks inspired my heart with her reading and fundamental notes on each of the ten personalities.

Carol Andrews took time to assist in writing the cover introduction. She had served with me as we ministered to youth who were behind prison bars.

I am most grateful to minister William Vasquez for reading and providing scriptural and paradoxical references to enrich reading categories.

I extend appreciation to Terry Nixon, Director of Operations for The Sentencing Project, for granting permission to use prison maps in this publication.

My heartfelt appreciation to Calvin Austin for sharing personal photos from his Tuskegee treasure chest.

I am most obliged to Donzella Maupin and Andreese Scott for the selection of photos of Booker T. Washington from the archives of Hampton University.

Before Leaving This Earth, Know Your PMA: Purpose, Mission, and Assignment could not have become a visual reality without your contribution.

Memories From Family Life in a Southern Tradition

This book is a direct result of my assignment to deliver my brother's eulogy in 2015. He was the one who encouraged me to develop my own gifts. "Stay in school, and make the honor roll, and do your best work!" he would say. He wanted me to be strong and to use my talents to help others. As I took my journey to college, I preserved those words in my heart.

As I traveled from Virginia by train, I thought seriously about the message I would present as the closing words on Joseph's life. He was the third and I am the fifth of twelve children. My mother trained my brother to manage the household in her absence. As I enjoyed the serene sites of nature—the trees, water, and animals—I realized what was most crucial in all of life was to know the purpose of your birth and why you were placed on this earth.

Oh, I visualized scenes from my childhood memories. I reflected on all the times my brother had guided us in activities that were so precious to us. We loved being under his supervision in the absence of our parents. He knew how to cook and to clean and how to care for the babies. My parents trained the eldest children to care for their younger siblings. There were no babysitters in the Southern culture. Parents taught their children the art of managing siblings in their absence. Any recalcitrant behavior reported would reap serious repercussions. The families in the community formed a close-knit bond. Any adult in the community could chastise children when they deviated from the neighborhood ethos. We were taught to respect our elders and to assist them in various activities.

My brother made life very interesting by engaging us in a variety of fun-filled activities during the day, and at the close of the day, he pretended to be Uncle Remus and kept us in suspense with a never-ending string of stories. My favorites were the tales he shared on holidays.

We busied ourselves with innumerable games and chores. Joseph gave us clear instructions when engaging us in these activities. We drew hearts to celebrate Valentine's Day, colored and designed eggs for our Easter egg hunts, and gloated over our new shorts and tops on the Fourth of July as we sat around the barbecue grill. Getting new sets of clothing always warmed our hearts. We would have fun modeling our outfits and received new clothes for Easter, the Fourth of July, and Christmas.

Oh, how we had to gear ourselves up to march back to the classroom the day after Labor Day. It was time to get back into the books, but three months later, we jubilantly celebrated Thanksgiving, fascinated by the tales of how the American natives taught the settlers to survive in a new land.

The most important holiday of the year for us was Christmas, and my brother engaged us in a variety of pre-Christmas activities, locating a tree in the woods to pulling names and buying gifts for our secretpartners. We had great fun helping our parents clean and decorate the house for this beautiful holiday. We learned to endure sacrifices, and when the holidays arrived, we were happily rewarded. We wore pants with knee patches and made do with resoled shoes. We mended our socks and sweaters. We internalized the value of making sacrifices and were willing to wait for newer items until there was room to accommodate them in the family budget. We were taught to embrace family and spiritual values. We were nurtured on adages, proverbs, and Benjamin Franklin's aphorisms. "Waste not, want not," "A stitch in time saves nine," and "A bird in the hand is better than two in the bush" are just some examples.

My brother encouraged us to do our best work in class and to participate in drama programs at church and in school. The church was the center of community life in the South, and children were involved in many training programs as well as drama presentations during the holidays. We memorized our parts for the church Christmas program as well as preparing ourselves for my mother's family enactment of the Christmas Story, which was always held on Christmas Eve.

The schools in the South gave us a two-week Christmas vacation. We used this time to take care of a myriad of chores to prepare for Christmas. My brother guided us in these family activities. He had a gift for turning chores into a source of fun. We accomplished a variety of tasks, cleaning the house, working in the yard, waxing linoleum rugs, and washing windows. With my brother's creativity, the linoleum rug became our skating rink. We used Johnson floor wax to prep the linoleum floor. We used old cloth to wrap our feet and create our skates. With all the fun, acrobatics, and competition, my mother soon had a shiny floor.

My brother assigned us to clean the windows in teams of two. One team member cleaned from the inside, and the other worked outside on the same window. The windows were prepped with Bon Ami window cleaner. When the paste dried, we began our work, identifying missed spots to our partners outside. Soon, my mother had clear bright windows.

The true joy came when my brother took us into the woods to select a Christmas tree. After making the selection, we stood back to let him cut the tree. Soon we were bringing our Christmas tree home. The next step was to find a large bucket or a pail. We packed the tree with soil. We were so happy and excited and could not wait to decorate the tree with colorful light bulbs and with decorations we had created.

The greatest fun after decorating the tree was pulling names. Everyone wrote his or her name on a strip of paper and folded the paper until it was very small. My brother instructed us to place our strips into a hat. Everyone was given an opportunity to pull one strip. Each of us would later purchase a Christmas gift for this secret mate and place it underneath the tree.

We had a cousin who was a great artist. Each year, we commissioned him to draw a big, beautiful picture of Santa Claus. We found places to display this art.

As we played with other kids in our neighborhood, we had favorite Christmas questions: "How many cakes will your mother bake? What do you want Santa to bring you? We were so proud of our window decorations. My mother and other parents in the community decorated their doors with Christmas wreaths and put candles inside each window.

The great joy was how everyone in Birmingham filled the air with Christmas. The radio station boomed with Christmas carols and songs throughout the day. The spirit of Christmas could be seen and heard throughout the streets of the community, but what we, as children, loved the most was the special radio broadcast hour. I especially recall listening one night when I was in the third grade. I had written my letter to Santa Claus, placed a three-cent stamp on my letter, and mailed it to the radio station. So every night my siblings and I were seated around the radio. And surely enough, my letter was read by Santa Claus. I had listed all the toys my siblings wanted—all twelve of us were included. And I can still hear my father's response as he listened to Santa read my letter: "Well, I guess I'd better get out and make sure Santa dreams come true."

Christmas was always a blessed time because it was filled with joy and happiness. My dad and my mother laid out gifts, toys, fruit, nuts, and candy for each one of us late on Christmas Eve. When we awakened on Christmas morning, we were the most joyous children around. We had bicycles, dolls, skates, doll beds—toys for everyone. I will cherish these memories in my heart forever.

My mother's Christmas program was second to none. There was much preparation for the program, to be performed on Christmas Eve. Each one of us was assigned a role to play. My mother and two younger sisters formed a great trio, who sang "Little Drummer Boy." My sister

Doris and I closed the program by acting out Clement C. Moore's poem, "'The Night Before Christmas." Doris and I worked in New York as teachers and we had so much fun dramatizing this poem. The house was filled with relatives, and the little children were out of their wits with excitement watching my sister and I open the windows and doors as if Santa were about to enter. It was so much fun that my sister and I had to stop in the middle of the performance to engage in laughter, too.

Of course, the traditional Christmas story was enacted and brought a spiritual reminder of the reason for the season. Afterwards, my mother invited all to the dining room table, which was laden with cakes, pies, pastries, and other holiday foods.

We kept busy singing Christmas carols, listening to great Christmas programs on the radio, and viewing wonderful human-interest stories on television. Unlike today, there were great stories with object lessons, instilling in us good morals for family and community living.

From my early childhood days, my parents gathered us around the fireplace to read the Bible to us and to share stories from their family histories. We learned to pray and to be reverent in any situation that might arise in life. I recall one family crisis very vividly. The doctor gave the dolorous news to my mother: "We have done all we can do for your husband. We don't know anything else to do." As my mother went about various duties, my brother carried on as our surrogate caretaker. He gave us the bad news, and he instructed us to gather around him in a family circle to pray. "We have to pray very hard because we may lose our dad and we will not have anyone to take care of us," he said.

Like most men, black and white, my father was employed at U.S. Steel. With solemn faces and bowed heads, we kneeled to pray. I can still recall this scene as if it had happened yesterday. Our prayers were answered, and my father was healed and worked for more than forty more years. He was able to pay off debt, serve in the church as a deacon, and see his children grow up.

As I reflect on these memories, I recall the legacy Joseph left with his own son and daughter. Joseph's wife was an educator. His daughter became an educational administrator, and his son is engaged in hotel management.

Delivering Joseph's message was easy because his life was filled with so many object lessons. As you read PMA, I urge you to take the opportunity to begin writing your own life's story before leaving this earth. Identify your unique purpose, passionately embrace your mission, and fulfill your special assignment.

I hope you will be both delighted and inspired by these charming mini biographies of ten historical figures who uplifted humanity with their gifts and talents.

PROLOGUE

The Origin of Sin (KJV)

God sends each individual into his world with a specific assignment. What were Jesus's purpose and assignment during the three decades plus three years he spent on this earth? Matthew 1:21 begins with the birth narrative. "And she shall bring forth a son, and thou shalt call his name JESUS: for he shall save his people from their sins."

"What sin?" is the question.

The question of the universe is, why did Adam and Eve disobey God? In Genesis 2:9, God gave the human pair a fruit variety. "And out of the ground made the Lord God to grow every tree that is pleasant to the sight, and good for food." With such a variety, why did the pair choose the path of disobedience?

As we turn to Genesis 3:1-3, we see the origin of the sin. "Now the serpent was more subtle than any beast of the field which the Lord God had made. And he said unto the woman, Yea, hath God said, Ye shall not eat of every tree of the garden? Eve, not being as crafty as the serpent, was easily lured into his lair. In her innocence, she was beguiled by the serpent. And the woman said unto the serpent, we may eat of the fruit of the trees of the garden. But of the fruit of the tree which is in the midst of the garden, God hath said, Ye shall not eat of it, neither shall ye touch it, lest ye die."

The serpent achieved two personal goals from his conversation with Eve. He caused Eve to doubt the instructions of God and planted curiosity in her mind. In Genesis 3:4, Satan said, "Ye shall not surely die." Knowing that Eve was almost convinced, Satan expanded his dialogue, being more deceitful in order to fill Eve with more doubt. "For God doth know that in the day ye eat thereof, then your eyes shall be opened, and ye shall be as gods, knowing good and evil" (Gen. 3:5).

What had Satan accomplished with Eve? Satan had enticed Eve to doubt the truth of God and to imagine herself being "a god" on par with the God of Creation instead of serving him. He was able to entice Adam and Eve in a single conversation. "And when the woman saw that the tree was good for food, and that it was pleasant to the eyes, and a tree to be desired to make one wise, she took of the fruit thereof, and did eat, and gave also unto her husband with her; and he did eat" (Gen. 3:6).

Eve and Adam were caught in Satan's lair and became fallen creatures of disobedience. The pair recognized Satan's chicanery as soon as they bit into the fruit from the forbidden Tree of Knowledge. "And the eyes of them both were opened, and they knew they were naked; and they sewed fig leaves together, and made themselves aprons" (Gen. 3:7).

The pair had taken the plunge into sin and was trying to hide from God. "And the Lord God called unto Adam, and said unto him, *Where art thou?"* (Gen. 3:9). God had one profound question for Adam. "Hast thou eaten of the tree, whereof I commanded thee that thou should not eat?" (Gen. 3:11)

Adam and Eve were beguiled by Satan, and each one received punishment. "And the Lord God said unto the serpent, because thou hast done this, thou art cursed above all cattle, and above every beast of the field; upon thy belly shalt thou go, and dust shalt thou eat all the days of thy life (Gen. 3:14): And I will put enmity between thee and the woman, and between thy seed and her seed; it shall bruise thy head, and thou shalt bruise his heel (Gen. 3:15). Unto the woman he said, I will greatly multiply thy sorrow and thy conception; and thy desire shall be to thy husband, and he shall rule over thee" (Gen. 3:16).

"And unto Adam he said, because thou hast hearkened unto the voice of thy wife, and hast eaten of the tree, of which I commanded thee, saying, Thou shalt not eat of it: cursed is the ground for thy sake; In sorrow shalt thou eat of it all the days of thy life (Gen. 3:17): Thorns also and thistles shall it bring forth to thee; and thou shalt eat the herb of the field (Gen. 3:18): In the sweat of thy face shalt thou eat bread, till thou return unto the ground; for out of it was thou taken: for dust thou art, and unto dust shalt thou return" (Gen. 3:19).

The sin of disobedience committed by Adam and Eve placed a curse upon the earth and humanity. This curse is referred to as the Fall of Man. Because of this, the first human pair could no longer remain in the garden where they had been contaminated. Their innocence was converted into a sin nature.

This *sin nature* was transmitted to all humanity. The holy estate of God was defiled by this sin. "So he drove out the man, and he placed at the east of the garden of Eden Cherubim, and a flaming sword which turned every way, to keep the way of the tree of life" (Gen. 3:24).

God in his mercy could have cast the human pair into hell and alienated them for an eternity, but because of his love for his creation, he provided a way to bring his creation back into his presence. The sin committed had to be redeemed. The redemption had to come through a perfect state of being, therefore, the God of Creation brought together the New Testament of the Bible. The New Testament reveals how humans are cleansed of sin through rebirth. The Book of John describes this gift of transformation that can be had through Jesus. "For God so loved the world that he gave his only begotten Son that whosoever believes in him shall not perish but have eternal life" (John 3:16).

Jesus, throughout his thirty-three years on earth, devoted his time to accomplishing his *purpose, mission,* and *assignment.* His mission was to continue the work until he had finished the course. The spiritual concept is described vividly by Paul. "I have fought a good fight, I have finished my course, I have kept the faith: Henceforth there is laid up for me a crown of righteousness, which the Lord, the righteous judge, shall give me at that day: and not to me only, but unto all them also that love his appearing" (2 Tim. 4:7-8).

Now that we know the sin and the gift of God to overcome the sin, we will focus on the need for each individual to fulfill his or her *purpose*, *mission*, and *assignment*.

INTRODUCTION

Our birth is but a sleep and a forgetting:
The Soul that rises with us, our life's Star,
  Hath had elsewhere its setting,
  And cometh from afar:
  Not in entire forgetfulness,
  And not in utter nakedness,
But trailing clouds of glory do we come
  From God, who is our home.
—William Wordsworth

How do we assess our being? When one looks around the ever-present world, how does one decide what one's role on this planet should be? How do we navigate the environs to find our place while living for a certain number of years without knowing the length of time that we will be given to be on this earth?

Oftentimes we depend upon parents and surrogates to guide us as we begin to steer our way through life, but a more nerve-racking question is, where did we have our beginning? Another great question before us is whether one comes with a blueprint at birth. Is there a magical plan that can tell us how to live this life that has been thrust upon each individual?

How to find one's purpose in life is a complicated question, and the answer, if found, would make a profound difference in how one would live his or her life. The self-assessment I will outline here consists of two parts. The first step is to identify your gifts and talents. Secondly, you will be asked to explore how these gifts are being used in your life. Ask yourself some questions: "What difference do I make in the lives of others when I share my gifts? What joys and emotions do I experience within my inner being?" This introspection will help you identify your purpose in life.

When I began making my own personal assessment, I realized I have a natural gift for making a positive impact on children. Through introspection I identified the things I liked and disliked about my childhood teachers. As I formed my philosophy of life, I wanted to embrace love and other values and integrate them into my teaching career. I valued kindness, understanding, an appreciation for individual differences, and an understanding of how learning styles vary from child to child. Above all, I wished to emphasize the reality that each individual is a special person with gifts that, when developed, could make a profound difference in uplifting humanity.

It was this identification of my gifts and my appreciation for them that helped me choose my career and embark upon my mission to impact society in a positive manner. My career preparation was in secondary education, counseling, administration, drama, and playwriting. After embarking on this career, I knew at the close of each day, I had touched the hearts of youth. By being in touch with the emotions at the heart of my inner being, I was able to make the correct career choice to fulfill my purpose in life.

As I have learned through my life experiences and can now see upon reflection, God has been at work since my childhood, molding and shaping me for my career. Consider, for example, my place in my family. Out of the twelve, I was the fifth born between six brothers. I was expected to take on the same responsibilities as the boys. Yet in my pre-teen years, I was taught to assist with my five younger sisters and two younger brothers. This responsibility helped me to develop a motherly, nurturing attitude as well as the ability to understand, inspire, and motivate children. It was easy for me to move from the Southland to teach an international population of children.

I had two primary lessons I wanted to impart. I wanted to teach them to love themselves, to love school, and I wanted to inspire them to develop their gifts and talents. When it was time for Open School, the parents were eager to meet the teacher who had so much influence on their children. When the holidays arrived, my students' faces shone with delight as they presented me with gifts. The secret to this kind of success is early recognition of what God has placed you on this earth to do.

Jesus was given his assignment before embarking on his life on earth. He was only twelve when, upon making a pilgrimage to Jerusalem, he recognized it was time for him to begin his ministry. Mary and Joseph had not internalized his age of reasoning. When they found him, after a day or two of searching for him among relatives, he was comfortably engaged in profound dialogue with the erudite men of that age. He recognized the time had come for him to begin the mission for which he was born.

Who am I and why was I born? Jesus's life mirrors the question! Jesus ministered to people from Galilee, Capernaum, Bethsaida, Nazareth, and across the village side. He taught them to live in community as he sat upon the mount. His messages lubricated and inspired the souls of men. He fed the five thousand, healed the sick, opened the eyes of the blind, and made the lame to walk, but at the close of the evening, Jesus found his way to the mountains, where he was alone. He took time to pray to God, his Father, and to restore himself.

Self-Assessment

To live 120 years without knowing and fulfilling **one's PMA is the saddest story ever to be told.** The most crucial part of life is identifying and achieving one's purpose for being born. I say to each and every one, "Before Leaving This Earth: Know Your PMA (Purpose, Mission and Assignment)"—the title of this book!

One cannot confuse a high income with one's purpose in life. Purpose is not synonymous with financial gain. When each of us identifies his or her purpose and works to fulfill it, we will come to know the joy of true happiness.

As an individualist, you will have the opportunity to make a self-assessment: Who am I? Why am I here on planet earth? You may find yourself asking, "Now that I am here, what am I to do as a person? What gifts lie inside me waiting to be born? How may I help to give them birth?" A more serious question is, "What must I do to make my gifts come alive to make a difference for myself and humanity?"

The key to achieving this lies within your heart and soul. We have been given these gifts in earthen vessels to use on God's earth to uplift humanity. The line of life reveals birth at one end of the continuum and death at the opposite end. One may ask two strategic questions: "Why have I been given these gifts?" and "How am I to use these gifts to take my journey in life between birth and death?"

I am sure the question reverberates somewhere in your soul. You might be thinking, "Yes, I have these gifts, and yes, I should develop these gifts as my golden package, but you may be driven to ponder something else as well. "Who am I to report to when I have come to the close of my life?" This self-examination should drive you to a quiet place where you can find solitude, and there you can begin the search into your inner being to find your purpose in life.

SELF-EXAMINATION

How do you see yourself on God's earth, and how can you use your talents? Take time to get in touch with your strengths and passions to help you decide what purpose God has in mind for you.

Some people earn seven- and eight-figure incomes, but despite their wealth, there is no peace in their souls. Instead, there may be great tension in the lives of these individuals. If one is perceived to be at the highest station in life, yet one does not experience happiness, there is conflict within the soul pleading to be resolved.

When one is unable to discern what is happening to him or her, there is a tendency to seek short-term solutions. This longing for answers and this search for inner fulfillment may affect one's social life or even drive an individual into a state of immoral behavior, which may give temporary relief but may also require one to increase the intensity of the pseudo crutch to assuage the inner suffering and pain.

You may recall stories of how some very talented people with great incomes became addicted to some vices in life that prevented them from using their gifts to uplift humanity. This is a very important phase in life. You want to guard against the exploitation or destruction of your gifts. We can cite one brief example, and you can probably think of others. One common scenario is when a great singer or musician is lured from a musical career in the church by a promise of fame, wealth, prestige, and a luxurious lifestyle for a brief period in their life. The person is, figuratively, on top of the world. However, lacking spiritual sagacity, he has missed the mark for completing his purpose, mission, and assignment. Material goods and fame cannot come to one's aid as he or she steps off the earth and stands before the Creator who loaned them the breath of life. The shutters close, the song is finished, and the dance steps shall be no more upon planet earth. You have been given these gifts and at the close of life, you are accountable for how your gifts were used.

How are you doing with your gifts? How many times have you completed your job, but within your inner being, there was still that quiet longing? This inner voice may be trying to nudge you to change the way you use your gifts and to find your purpose in life.

When you are undergoing these experiences, you may want to remember the ONE whose breath you share daily—the God of Creation. This would be a good time to begin to nourish your spirit with the living God. As you take time to embrace various facets of your life, you may reserve solo time with the Creator—the One who made you, knows you, loves you, and has already designed a blueprint for your life. Think about what God told Jeremiah: "Before I formed thee in the belly I knew thee; and before thou came forth out of the womb, I sanctified thee, and I ordained thee a prophet unto the nations" (Jer. 1:5). What was God's assignment to Jeremiah? God appointed Jeremiah to be a prophet to the nations. Just as God gave an assignment to Jeremiah, he also has designed a purpose for your life. As you work to fulfill that mission, you will find inner peace.

We can recall the story of Jonah, a biblical prophet from the Old Testament. He tried very hard to circumvent God's will. Besides being disobedient and refusing to travel to Nineveh as God had instructed him to do, he chose to follow his own course. He was going as far away from this city as possible. And surely, he was not going to preach a message to a people he despised. He, therefore, took a voyage of his own choosing on a small ship. Why would he try to preach to an immoral population? No way! He was not going to obey that request.

Some of you know this story. Jonah went his own way and chose to take a ship to Joppa instead of obeying God. Of course, he had forgotten that God is not only omniscient (knowing all things) but is also omnipresent—present everywhere. When the ship was caught in a terrible storm, the captain of the ship importuned everyone to begin praying to their god to save them. Jonah had found a comfortable place to sleep. The crew was very frightened and immediately awakened Jonah.

"Can't you see the storm?" one cried. " We are about to perish! Get up and pray to your god that we may be spared." Old Jonah knew God had brought the storm to let him know he could not hide, but he pretended to be innocent. Finally, when there was no relief, he volunteered the truth to the crew. "Throw me off the ship," he said, "and calm will return to the waters."

When the men realized no amount of their work would save the ship, they took Jonah at his word and threw him into the deep. As soon as this deed was done, the sea returned to a state of calm. Jonah was quickly swallowed up by a whale, in whose belly he spent three days, offering prayers to God in acknowledgment of his sin. Finally, the Lord heard his prayer and permitted the whale to regurgitate him onto the shore.

A happy man, relieved of his disobedience and remorse, Jonah traveled to that place where he had not wished to go. He preached God's message to those sinful people. When the king heard the message, he sent out a decree across the land. "God is displeased with our sinful behavior, and if we do not repent, acknowledge our sins and ask forgiveness, this whole nation and lovely city will be destroyed. Get out of your fineries, dress up in sackcloth and get down and pray to the Lord, lest we all perish together," were the king's words. When God saw the people humbled in repentance and dressed in sackcloth, he had a change of heart. Their adherence to the king's edict saved the people and the beautiful city.

Where are you today? The God of yesterday is also the God of today. We were each placed on this earth for a purpose and given an assignment to help us fulfill a mission. I will share with you the stories of ten people who not only found their purposes in life but met the challenges that confronted them as each sought to fulfill his or her purpose, assignment, and mission. As you read these biographical sketches, you may recognize similar challenges in your own life, but like these persons, you too, through hard work and perseverance, will be happy that you pursued the work God assigned you to do between birth and death—to make a positive difference on God's earth and go home to a soldier's reward.

CHAPTER I

JOHN THE BAPTIST

Repent, the kingdom of God is at hand.
Themes: Out of darkness
            Walk in the light.
            Guide us to the path of peace.
Place: The Jordan River
Time: The time of Christ, AD

Purpose

John was the forerunner of Jesus, who preached the message of repentance from sin and beckoned all to turn to God for forgiveness.

Mission

John preached salvation to all who would listen. He had a single mission—to tell the people to repent of their sins and live by the Word of God. John did not conform to this world. The world's materialism neither attracted him nor distracted him from fulfilling his mission. He was not lured by the trappings of high society and wealth. He did not dress in the fineries that some people of importance saw as a form of validation. The wilderness preacher was not attracted to designer fashion; he dressed in camel hair with his loins clad in a leathern girdle. He did not seek fine dining in exquisite palaces and homes. He was happy and satisfied with his natural diet of locusts and honey and certainly did not indulge in caviar and champagne (Matt. 3:4).

Courage

John's focus was on his mission, and he had the courage to fulfill it. He did not value the opinions of people over his mission. He did not alter his mission to win praise. When the Roman soldiers, the Pharisees, and the scribes came into his wilderness territory, he preached the same message to them that he did to others. "But when he saw many Pharisees and Sadducees come to his baptism, he said unto them, O generation of vipers, who hath warned you to flee from the wrath to come" (Matt. 3:7)?

John did not seek any political favors. *He simply spoke truth to all under divine authority.* His mission was strictly focused on the message of repentance and baptism, and he did not embrace glory for himself. "I indeed baptize you with water unto repentance: but he that cometh after me is mightier than I, whose shoes I am not worthy to bear: he shall baptize you with the Holy Ghost, and with fire" (Matt. 3:11). *John delivered a divine message and never lost focus on the Divine.*

Fortitude

He accosted Herod for his immorality. The king had married Herodias, his brother Philip's wife. "For Herod had laid hold on John, and bound him, and put him in prison for Herodias' sake, his brother Philip's wife" (Matt. 14:3). This bold preaching led to the beheading of John the Baptist.

Divine Connection

The work of John was divine, and his mission was set forth at birth. His parents, Zacharias and Elizabeth, had been without child. Zacharias's prayers ascended to heaven, and God responded. "But the angel [Gabriel] said unto him, Fear not, Zacharias: for thy prayer is heard; and thy wife Elizabeth shall bear thee a son, and *thou shalt call his name John*" (Luke 1:13).

Persistence

There was no threat, no bribe, and no favor that could deter John's mission. He could not be lured into favoritism within the power structure of his day. Under God's divine order, John remained faithful until his death. One verse that defines his work and persistence is Romans 8:39. "Nor height, nor depth, nor any other creature, shall be able to separate us from the love of God, which is in Christ Jesus our Lord." The trailblazer, with a mission, remained fearlessly focused until his work was completed.

Faith

From the womb, John the Baptist was anointed in faithfulness to Christ. When Mary went to visit her cousin, Elizabeth, who was six months into her pregnancy, scripture tells us that the infant John leaped in his mother's womb. "And it came to pass, that, when Elizabeth heard the salutation of Mary, the babe leaped in her womb; and Elizabeth was filled with the Holy Ghost" (Luke: 1:41). The greeting was a threefold circle. Elizabeth rejoiced, Mary rejoiced, and baby John leaped with joy.

John's abiding faith was exemplified in his mission. He turned neither left nor right, but moving straight ahead, he pursued his assignment. He was "a voice crying in the wilderness, Prepare ye the way of the Lord, make his paths straight" (Matt. 3:3).

Talents and Gifts

Firstly, John was a truth speaker—a powerful orator who commanded the attention of all people from the lowly to the powerful. Herod acknowledged John's spiritual gift by showing remorse for making a covenant with the daughter of Herodias for the beheading of John. "And the king was sorry: nevertheless for the oath's sake, and them which sat with him at meat, he commanded it to be given her" (Luke 14:9).

The king (Herod the Tetrarch) at his birthday celebration requested his wife's daughter to dance and "promised with an oath to give her whatsoever she would ask" (Matt. 14:7). He had no idea the daughter of Herodias would request the head of John the Baptist. The dancer consulted with her mother and asked her to name the prize. Her mother was annoyed, on a daily basis, with John's messages categorizing her marriage as adultery. It was true she had previously been married to Philip, the king's brother, but she had grown weary of John's constant talk about it. Therefore, the young daughter, after consultation with her mother, gave her request to the king: "I want John the Baptist's head on a platter."

The king was in great remorse. He had no idea she would make this request. He was surrounded by his courtiers, and could not rescind his words. In truth, the king admired John's bold preaching in the wilderness.

When Jesus heard of the imprisonment and death of John, he saluted the wilderness preacher. "Verily I say unto you, Among them that are born of women there hath not risen a greater than John the Baptist" (Matt. 11:11).

CHAPTER 2

JESUS: THE REDEEMER

Theme: A gift from God to provide salvation to humanity
Place: Bethlehem
Time: Birth of Jesus, 1 AD

Purpose

Jesus is the fulfillment of the promises proclaimed by John in the Jordan River. Christ came to fulfill the mission of God, to realize the work of John, and to offer salvation to humanity.

Mission

JESUS was sent into the world by the God of Creation to offer salvation to restore a broken humanity back to God. He gathered twelve men to spread this great message of redemption. His mission was replete. He taught, healed, and bound the wounds of people near and far. "Ye have heard that it hath been said, Thou shalt love thy neighbor, and hate thine enemy. But I say unto you, love your enemies, bless them that curse you, do good to them that hate you, and persecute you; That ye may be the children of your Father which is in heaven: for he makes his sun to rise on the evil and on the good, and sends rain on the just and on the unjust. For if ye love them which love you, what reward have ye? Do not even the publicans the same? Be ye therefore perfect, even as your Father which is in heaven is perfect" (Matt. 5:43-48).

Courage

The most powerful reality of Jesus is expressed in John 5:30. "I can of mine own self do nothing: as I hear, I judge: and my judgment is just; because I seek not mine own will, but the will of the Father which hath sent me." Jesus was repetitive when expressing and explaining his purpose for being on earth. "And the Father himself, which hath sent me, hath borne witness of me" (John 5:37). When he was confronted with earthly principalities, Jesus always remembered the power of God, who had sent him. "And he that sent me is with me: the Father hath not left me alone; for I do always those things that please him" (John 8:29).

Fortitude

Jesus was fortified in his mission to obey the will of God. "My meat is to do the will of him that sent me, and to finish the work" (John 4:34). Throughout his ministry, Jesus held steadfastly to his mission of obeying the will of God. "Therefore, doth my Father love me, because I lay down my life, that I might take it again" (John 10:17). Finally, he completed the victory through his crucifixion, death, and resurrection. In John 17, we find the most beautiful verse in the Bible: "I have glorified thee on earth: I have finished the work which thou gave me to do" (John 17:4). The passage then continues: "And now, O Father, glorify thou me with thine own self with the glory which I had with thee before the world was" (John 17:5).

The truth of creation is revealed in Genesis 1:26. "Let us make man in our image, after our likeness." He was with God in the beginning, and now Jesus has completed the divine work to fulfill his mission and return to the God of Creation.

Divine Connection

John 3:16 reveals the divine plan to give humanity a path to God through the crucifixion, death, and resurrection of Jesus. God revealed the divinity of Jesus at his baptism in the Jordan River. "And Jesus, when he was baptized, went up straightway out of the water: and lo, the heavens were opened unto him: And lo a voice from heaven, saying, "This is my beloved Son, in whom I am well pleased" (Matt. 3:16-17). Throughout his ministry on earth, Jesus was in constant communication with God. At the close of his work on a daily basis, he retreated to the mountains to find renewal by spending quiet time with God.

Persistence

Jesus's ministry was consistent. He alone knew the will of the Father. When the people in various towns petitioned him to remain, he always remembered his mission. In one such case, he revealed a profound truth about humanity. *He was not biased toward one group at the expense of others.* When one crowd petitioned him to stay longer in their town, he responded with these words: "And other sheep I have, which are not of this fold: them also I must bring, and they shall hear my voice, and there shall be one fold, and one shepherd" (John 10:16).

From the manger to the cross, Jesus knew his *purpose, assignment,* and completed his *mission.* While on the cross, he spoke his dying words, "Father, forgive them; for they know not what they do" (Luke 23-34). Jesus opened the door for humanity to come to him to overcome their sin nature.

Faith

Jesus's faith demonstrated perfect submission to the God of Creation. "My sheep hear my voice, and I know them, and they follow me: And I give unto them eternal life; and they shall never perish, neither shall any man pluck them out of my hand" (John 10:27-28). *His faith and his mission were inextricably tied to God.* "My Father, which gave them me, is greater than all; and no man is able to pluck them out of my Father's hand" (John 10:29).

Talents and Gifts

John 10:30 defines the gifts and talents of Jesus. "*I and my Father are one.*" There are absolutely no impossibilities for Jesus. Healing the sick, opening the eyes of the blind, making the lame to walk, and raising the dead all were things he did. *His gifts are derived from the God of Creation—replete without error and without end.*

Jesus ministered to people from Galilee, Capernaum, Bethsaida, Nazareth, and across the village side. He taught them to live in community as he sat upon the mount. His messages stirred the souls of men, women, boys, and girls. Once, when parents were trying to get through the crowd to have their children blessed by Jesus, they were prohibited from doing so by some of his disciples. Jesus looked upon the crowd to correct this behavior, telling them, "Suffer the little children to come unto me and forbid them not: for of such is the kingdom of God" (Mark 10:14).

Jesus worked each day. He fed the five thousand, healed the sick, opened the eyes of the blind, and made the lame to walk. He knew God had sent him into this world, and he knew the *purpose* and *mission* that characterized his work on this earth. You, too, can spend time with the Lord so he can circumcise and prune your heart that you may grow to understand your *purpose* and your *assignment* on this earth. When you realize your purpose, you will begin to experience true happiness. "Yea, happy is that people, whose God is LORD" (Ps. 144:15).

SCRIPTURES
The Great Commission Matthew 28:19-20
I am the way, the truth, and the life. John 14:6
The world hated me; it will hate you. John 15:18
I have overcome the world. John 16:33

There is only one mediator. I Timothy 2:5
God so loved the world John 3:16
Father, forgive them. Luke 23:34

CHAPTER 3

ABIGAIL ADAMS

A Portrait of God: Love for Family, Community, and Humanity

Theme: God's model for his world—family, community, humanity, and his law
Time: The American Revolution (1775–1783) through the War of 1812
Born: November 11, 1744
Died: October 28, 1818, in Weymouth, Massachusetts
Married John Adams

Abigail Adams was the daughter of a preacher; her mother worked tirelessly in the community ministering to the infirm and others in need. Certainly, Abigail's history may have played a role in molding and shaping her into the woman she became. Most women of her time did not have the privilege of receiving an education. However, Abigail's father had a library, and this made a difference in her life. She enjoyed reading and spent a great deal of time digesting books on various subjects. The balance in her life may have developed from a close working relationship with her mother. Abigail was a vibrant young teenager who treasured the time she spent with her mother traveling through the community as they ministered to the infirmed and impoverished population. Abigail developed a caring spirit for those from all walks of life.

Being a well-read and well-bred young lady, she engaged family guests in broad conversations on various subjects, problems, and issues of the revolutionary era. One young man who was greatly attracted to Abigail was John Adams. After a brief courtship, they were married in 1764.

These were tumultuous times for the thirteen colonies as they pondered their grievances against England. By 1776, the Declaration of Independence had been drawn up and delivered to England. John Adams was a mainstay in this battle leading to the revolution and culminating with independence for the United States of America. Abigail worked side by side with John as his confidant and wife. She was an extraordinary woman who flavored her conversation with poetry, philosophy, and politics. Through her daily written communication, Abigail contributed to the work of building the new government, sharing her ideas on how to resolve many of the political challenges and problems. John looked forward to receiving her inspiring letters. Some kind historians have, affectionately, designated her as one of the Founding Fathers. By 1774, Abigail and John had five children. The amount of strength and wisdom Abigail possessed was incredible.

She is highlighted in this publication because of her strength, wisdom, courage, and love for her husband. She was his helpmate and gave him moral support as he worked assiduously as a Founding Father. Abigail had a true love for humanity. Just as she voiced her opinion that the slaves were entitled to freedom, she expressed support for the rights of women. John frequently sought the advice of Abigail on many matters. On one such occasion, she lifted her voice on behalf of women. "If particular care and attention is not paid to the ladies, we are determined to foment a rebellion, and will not hold ourselves bound by any laws in which we have no voice, or representation," she said. [1]

Purpose

Abigail was her husband's closest advisor in shaping the framework of the United States Constitution and setting the foundation for the new nation. The couple had many intellectual discussions on politics and government. The young nation was confronted with a myriad of problems after winning its independence. The nations in Europe were slow to recognize America as a nation and often disrespected the new country. Although France was an ally to the USA, many Frenchmen who resided in America were causing dissension. Abigail supported her husband's political career and supported policies such as the Alien and Sedition Acts in 1798. "The Alien Act gave the President the power to deport aliens or foreigners. The Sedition Act made it a crime for anyone to publish 'any false, scandalous, and malicious writing about the President, Congress, or national government." [2] Abigail played her role well as the wife of the second president and later as the mother of President John Quincy Adams

Mission

Abigail had to manage the farm and household as well as teaching and training the children in her husband's absence while he fulfilled a vital role in Philadelphia forming the foundation of the new nation. Just a few of her responsibilities included prepping the land for spring planting and fall harvesting and securing local help for breaking the ground, seeding, watering, and weeding. Gathering and maintaining household supplies and making house repairs were simple everyday challenges. She had to supervise the children's schoolwork and Bible study, assigning tasks and chores and making sure that peace and harmony were maintained in the family. In addition, she had to protect her children from the temptations of immoral pathways and maintain a prayer life with them.

Courage

Indomitable courage! Abigail and John lived in Massachusetts. John spent long periods of time away from Abigail assisting in the writing of the Articles of Confederation, which were the first written form of government in America. Later he spent time away in Philadelphia helping to form the Constitution.

There were so many challenging years for Abigail. She gave birth to most of their children while John was away to handle crises or while he was busy writing and debating laws that would govern the new nation. She had to manage the farm and the children in his absence. Despite these challenging responsibilities, she found time to write inspiring letters to John on a daily basis. This correspondence is archived for future generations to read.

Fortitude

Abigail had love and compassion for her husband and the work he had committed himself to do for the nation, but she faced enduring challenges as the head of the household in his absence. She gave birth to six children and had to cope with the stillbirth of a daughter she named Elizabeth. My own mother shared with me the heartache of delivering a stillborn child after carrying the baby full term. I can imagine how Abigail, too, suffered from this personal loss.

Managing a household can be very challenging. She shared some of her struggles with her son Charles, who became addicted to alcohol and died at the age of thirty. When her husband was elected as the second president of the nation, she brought Charles's daughter, Susanna, who was just three, to live with them in the White House.

Divine Connection

Abigail's faith sustained her through troubling and challenging times. She not only suffered the loss of her stillborn baby but also lost her daughter Nabby, to breast cancer.

In addition to experiencing the joy of being the wife of the second president of the United States, she had the honor of seeing her son John Quincy Adams become the sixth president.

Persistence

A soliloquy may have helped her find inner strength.

"John is away from me for long periods of time, but I will stay the course. I will honor my vows of marriage and remain faithful to him. I must assist him in fulfilling his purpose in life. It is not all about me. As the great poet Kahlil Gibran noted in his book *The Prophet*, it is the recognition of each in the marriage bond, to fulfill their mission in life. We are in this marriage together to help each other accomplish our assignments in life. We will help and encourage each other."

Abigail would have loved to have had her husband present throughout her married years, but she had to sacrifice much time to the Founding Fathers. When the colonies drew up the Declaration of Independence in 1776, Abigail had given birth between 1765 to 1777. She had the courage to persist in John's absence, and her strength and her faith in the Lord gave her the willpower to stay strong during her travails.

Faith

Foundations built in Abigail's childhood set the pattern for her adult life. She had faith not only in her family, children, and friends but in humanity as well. She wanted the thirteen colonies to win in their fight for freedom and become a strong new nation.

I believe the most precious part of Abigail's faith was evident in her position regarding the slaves in the colonies. She was a bold woman who stood for truth and justice in her time. Thomas Jefferson, in his first draft of the Declaration of Independence, accused England of forcing slavery upon the colonies, writing, "He has waged cruel war against human nature itself, violating its most sacred rights of life and liberty in the persons of a distant people who never offended him, captivating and carrying them into slavery in another hemisphere, or to incur miserable death in their transportation thither."[3]

The Southern colonies rejected the original version of the Declaration of Independence. They wanted to retain slavery in the colonies. Abigail, however, took a Christian stand. She spoke vehemently against the colonies that did not want to free the slaves during the fight against England for independence. She wrote, "It always appeared a most iniquitous scheme to me to fight ourselves for what we are daily robbing and plundering from those who have as much a right to freedom as we have."[4]

Talents and Gifts

Abigail Adams was a gifted writer and used this gift to motivate and inspire her husband as he endured the challenging times they faced. She was greatly adept at supervising both the farm and the household. Her gifts and her love for family made all the difference in her ability to embrace her purpose in life.

Summary

Abigail took on her assignment in life and wasted no time in fulfilling her mission. God gave her nurturing parents to prepare her for her role in life. As a great helpmate and advisor to John, she made it possible for him to fulfill an important role as a Founding Father.

John was elected as the nation's second president and occupied the first executive mansion on Market Street in Philadelphia from March 1797 to May 1800.[5] On November 1, 1800, the current White House was completed. Abigail and John were the first presidential pair to reside in Washington, D.C. They had toiled through the various stages of establishing the thirteen colonies as the United States of America. The mission was complete, and they were rewarded by becoming the first couple to grace America's White House. John Adams's most famous quotation is, *"Posterity! You will never know, how much it cost the present Generation, to preserve your Freedom! I hope you will make a good Use of it. If you do not, I shall repent in Heaven, that I ever took half the Pains to preserve it."*

Letter from John Adams to Abigail Adams, 26 April 1777
Saturday Evening 26 April 1777[6]

I have been lately more remiss, than usual in Writing to you. There has been a great Dearth of News. Nothing from England, nothing from France, Spain, or any other Part of Europe, nothing from the West Indies. Nothing from Howe, and his Banditti, nothing from General Washington.

There are various Conjectures that **Lord Howe** is dead, sick, or gone to England, as the Proclamation run in the Name of Will. Howe only, and nobody from New York can tell any Thing of his Lordship.

I am wearied out, with Expectations that the Massachusetts Troops would have arrived, e'er now, at Head Quarters. — Do our People intend to leave the Continent in the Lurch? Do they mean to submit? Or what Fatality attends them? With noblest Prize in View, that ever Mortals contended for, and with the fairest Prospect of obtaining it upon easy Terms, The People of the Massachusetts Bay, are dead.

Does our State intend to send only half, or a third of their Quota? Do they wish to see another, crippled, disastrous and disgraceful Campaign for Want of an Army? – I am more sick and more ashamed of my own Countrymen, than ever I was before. The Spleen, the Vapors, the Dismals, the Horrors, seem to have seized our whole State.

More Wrath than Terror, has seized me. I am very mad. The gloomy Cowardice of the Times, is intolerable in N. England.

Indeed I feel not a little out of Humour, from Indisposition of Body. You know, I cannot pass a Spring, or fall, without an ill Turn – and I have had one these four or five Weeks – a Cold, as usual. Warm Weather, and a little Exercise, with a little Medicine, I suppose will cure me as usual. I am not confined, but moap about and drudge as usual. I am a

Fool if ever there was one to be such a Slave. I wont be much longer. I will be more free, in some World or other.

Is it not intolerable, that the opening Spring, which I should enjoy with my Wife and Children upon my little farm, should pass away, and laugh at me, for labouring, Day after Day, and Month after Month, in a Conclave, Where neither Taste, nor Fancy, nor Reason, nor Passion, nor Appetite can be gratified?

Posterity! You will never know, how much it cost the present Generation, to preserve your Freedom! I hope you will make a good Use of it. If you do not, I shall repent in Heaven, that I ever took half the Pains to preserve it.

CHAPTER 4

HARRIET TUBMAN

Proclaim liberty throughout the land.
Leviticus 23:10

Theme: A passage to liberty for runaway slaves—The Underground Railroad
Place: The United States of America
Time: 1822–1865
Born: 1822 in Dorchester, Maryland
Died: March 10, 1913, in Auburn, New York, at the age of 90 or 91

Purpose

Harriet Tubman was born to guide her people to freedom.

Her early life included an accident that may have set the mold for her life. She suffered a traumatic head wound when an irate slave owner threw a heavy metal weight, intending to hit another slave but hitting her instead. It is believed by some physicians that she may have suffered temporal lobe epilepsy as a result of the injury.[1]

Harriet also began to experience strange visions and vivid dreams, which she saw as being premonitions from God. She looked to God to direct her actions throughout her life.

She escaped to Philadelphia in 1849 and began returning to Maryland to guide dozens of other slaves to freedom. She traveled in extreme secrecy, having devised a way for slaves to steal away from the plantation on a secret path, traveling by night and hiding out by day. This method of traveling was known as the Underground Railroad. Harriet was so successful with her Freedom Train that she was given the nickname "Moses." After the Fugitive Slave Act of 1850 became law, she planned a trail into Canada.

Mission

Harriet Tubman endured the shackles and the hardships of slavery. Her master rented her out to various plantations, but once she realized she had been born for the purpose of leading her people to freedom, this revelation became a guidepost pointing to her future. She would no longer live as a slave on God's earth, and she greatly internalized this concept of freedom. When her husband, John Tubman, a free man, did not embrace her vision, she kept her thoughts of freedom close to her heart. She realized when one has a goal, it may be necessary to walk alone, but in her quest to be free, she did not feel she was alone. Within her heart, she felt the presence of divine hands guiding her pathway to freedom. As she embraced her mission, she let nothing deter her. No, it was not an easy journey, but she tied her few belongings into a knapsack and carried also the spiritual qualities she would also need—tenacity, persistence, strength, courage, and faith. When challenges appeared to be insurmountable, Harriet reached into her philosophy of life and grabbed golden nuggets that inspired her heart and kept her faith strong as she continued on the journey that had been personally designed by God.

Harriet Tubman found freedom and discovered her mission in life. She was not satisfied with securing her own freedom; she wanted to help others achieve liberty. That golden light in her heart directed her to devise a plan to pursue this mission until the Civil War had culminated with the passage of the Thirteenth Amendment to abolish slavery in the United States.

Courage

Courage may have been invented by Harriet Tubman! She had incredible fortitude. As a slave who was hired out by her master on assignments, Harriet was a woman of great bravery. Historians paint her as a woman who worked as hard as any man. Tired of laboring like a beast of burden, she meditated on the day she would escape from Anthony Thompson's plantation in Maryland.

One day, Harriet decided to make her dream a reality. Unable to receive help from her husband to plot her escape, Harriet took the path of a lone warrior. Upon arriving in Philadelphia in 1849, Harriet could not believe she had reached Freedom Land. "When I found I had crossed that line," she said, "I looked at my hands to see if I was the same person. There was such a glory over everything; the sun came like gold through the trees, and over the fields, and I felt like I was in Heaven."[2]

Fortitude

Harriet worked many days on the Thompson plantation, but when she heard the voice of the Lord inspiring her heart to design a plan for freedom, she was obedient. She concluded that God did not want her to remain a slave. She took courage and ran away. Arriving in Philadelphia, Harriet realized her dream, but in her heart reverberated a desire to make freedom available to others. Like Jeremiah, who received his assignment from God at birth, Harriet was determined to realize her mission to guide other slaves from the brutal life of bondage. She designed her plan for her Freedom Train. She plotted and memorized the various stopovers and places for escape that were accessible to her. This fortitude and great faith in the Lord enabled Harriet to go down in history as the "Moses" of her people through her work as the conductor of the Underground Railroad. In her love for the Lord, she always prayed and gave thanks to God for aid from Quakers and other people who were known to be abolitionists. The work of these abolitionists paved the road to the Civil War. The number of people opposing slavery increased, and the fury against this peculiar institution grew, while conscientious legislators work tirelessly in Congress. The Civil War ensued between 1861 to 1865. Finally, the Thirteenth Amendment to end slavery became a reality in 1865.

Divine Connection

The conductor of the Underground Railroad did not walk alone. She was nurtured in faith by her parents, Ben and Rit. It is believed her mother had been taken from the Ashanti tribe in Ghana, West Africa, and brought to America. Ben and Rit had nine children, and they shared both their history and their faith with their offspring.[3]

When Harriet sustained her head injury, no one expected her to live. Ben and Rit worked day and night to nurse their daughter, who was fading in and out of consciousness. They continued their prayers and used herbs and various remedies, hoping to save her life. Finally, Harriet recovered, but a change had come over her, and it remained with her throughout her life. Without warning, she would fall into a long and deep sleep. Upon awakening, she shared visions she had seen in her dreams. She embraced these experiences as her time with the Lord. These visions became a divine guide in her life as she conducted the Underground Railroad and also inspired her in her work after the Civil War and until her death.

Persistence

Persistence is the quality of completing a task or a goal in life. Despite trials and tribulations, one must have the stamina to stay the course. Harriet Tubman internalized this concept and applied it to her life. She embraced her God-given assignment to direct her Freedom Train. Despite the dangers, threats, and the bounties placed on her head, she persevered. There are many stories about how she devised ways to gain freedom for others.

One instance of her resourcefulness took place when Harriet was on an assignment to take some slaves from her old master's plantation. She had to be extremely cautious because there was a $300 bounty on her head. When she arrived in Maryland, she immediately recognized her old master and quickly came up with a way to disguise herself. Dressed as an old woman with a cane and a basket of chickens, she pulled off the ruse. She opened the basket to free the chickens and began running after them. As her master passed, he giggled in delight, calling "Git 'hem, Granny, git 'hem!" It was a close call, but the conductor of the Underground Railroad had accomplished her goal. She would not let anything deter her from her life's mission.

On another trip, Harriet had a half dozen freedom seekers with her on a rescue mission. She had previously given warnings about the struggles of their journey. After walking about half the way, one passenger lost courage and wanted to turn back. If he had, the result would have been lost lives. Harriet travelled with a shotgun. When she heard the passenger talk about his plans, she pointed her gun directly at his face, terrifying everyone and saying "If you turn back, I will blow your head off your shoulders!" Harriet's feat of delivering more than three hundred passengers safely into Freedom Land made her the "Moses of her people."

Faith

Harriet was a woman of faith and a warrior for her beliefs, a role which she embraced in her daily walk. Slave masters had great political influence. They used this power to lobby for the passage of the 1850 Fugitive Slave Act. This law stipulated that if slaves had stolen their way into the North, it would be the responsibility of northerners to return them to the South. The laying of this cobblestone helped to pave the road to the Civil War. Northerners were irate at the passage of this act. This new law posed a great threat to Harriet and her Underground Railroad. She put thought into her next step but looked mainly to her faith for ways to overcome this new obstacle. Her system of traveling with fugitives by night and hiding in the day with the cooperation of Quakers and other friends would now be destroyed by this legislation, but by faith the Underground conductor came up with a new way of guiding her passengers to freedom. She trusted God to provide an extended route all the way into Canada. Hebrews 11:1 describes faith as "the substance of things hoped for, the evidence of things not seen." Increasing the miles she was able to travel in her rescue work, she continued to safely operate her Underground Railroad.

Talents

Harriet Tubman identified and used her gifts and talents to embrace her assignment, complete her mission, and fulfill her purpose in life.

She is renowned as the conductor of the Underground Railroad. When we study her biography, we learn she was a woman of many talents. She was a humanitarian, an abolitionist, and a spy in the US army as well as a cook. She worked in the Union army as a cook and nurse. She was also the first woman to lead an armed expedition in the Civil War.

Summary

The creator of the underground passage pursued her purpose with courage. Having gained freedom for herself, she devised a plan to help hundreds of other slaves escape to the North. After the passage of the Fugitive Slave Law of 1850, the conductor continued her mission, guiding runaways to Canada.

Harriet was a woman of great wit. She relocated her parents to Canada, and the winters were very cold. In 1859, she was blessed to be able to purchase a piece of property in Auburn, New York, from Senator William H. Seward. Seward was a Republican and famed abolitionist. The property served many purposes for Harriet. It was a haven for her family and friends. Throughout the year, she took in boarders and offered a safe place for blacks who were seeking a better life in the North.[4]

At the beginning of her search for freedom, Harriet had to leave her first husband. Later, she met Nelson Charles Davis, and they were married in 1869. Davis was a North Carolina native who had served in the 8th U.S. Colored Infantry from 1863 to 1865. He worked in Auburn as a brick layer. They remained married until his death in 1888.[5]

Harriet continued her work to achieve social justice and equality until her death on March 10, 1913. It had been a long journey from life as a little slave girl, born in Maryland, to finding freedom in Philadelphia and extending the Underground Railroad into Canada. Harriet's persistence, fueled by faith, allowed her to complete her mission.

CHAPTER 5

THADDEUS STEVENS

A Voice for Freedom in the Fight Against American Slavery

Theme: Freedom for all humanity
Place: US Congress and State Legislatures
Time: Nineteenth Century
Born: April 4, 1792
Died: August 11, 1868

How did Thaddeus Stevens come to identify his purpose in life? What could have led Stevens to pursue his mission? Sometimes a clue to identifying one's purpose in life can be found in his or her birth circumstances or early childhood. Stevens was the second of the four sons of Joshua and Sarah Stevens. He was born with a clubfoot and had a brother who was born with two clubfeet. When the youngest son was twelve, the children were deserted by their father. As the head of the household, their mother worked several jobs to ensure a quality education for her boys, even if it meant moving to another town. Sarah instilled in Stevens a well-defined concept of purpose and taught him to believe he was just as good as anyone else. Stevens developed a strong sense of self-worth in grammar school. He ignored taunts from his classmates. Sometimes he made a great spectacle of himself by placing his clubfoot on top of his desk. He would not let that foot deter him from accomplishing his life's ambition.[1] He was going to become a lawyer.

Assignment

Stevens completed Caledonia Grammar School, known as Peacham Academy. In 1814, he graduated from Dartmouth College.[2] His path continued to unfold for him. He began his study of law with Judge John Mattocks in Danville. Stevens kept his eyes opened for career opportunities. Through correspondence with friends, he acquired some information that led him to relocate to Pennsylvania in 1815. Sometimes one's mission in life may require one to travel. A look at God's instructions to Abraham in Genesis 12:1 gives us an example. "Now the Lord had said unto Abram, get thee out of thy country, and from thy kindred, and from thy father's house, unto a land that I will show thee." Stevens was willing to move to pursue his goal and life mission.

He wasted no time in making his decision to relocate to Pennsylvania. He continued his law studies while teaching school at the York Academy. It was rumored that local lawyers had passed a resolution barring any students who had not practiced law for two consecutive years from taking the bar exam. During this period of history, various laws were enacted to hinder or prevent certain people from entering certain professions, sometimes because of physical appearances and similarly shallow reasons. Stevens would let nothing obstruct his career pathway. Sometimes class- and status-related roadblocks may be set up for the purpose of preserving exclusivity. Stevens's physical challenges may have categorized him in the minds of others, but he had a mission to fulfill. He circumvented this obstruction [which he believed was put into place because of his physical condition] by entering the exam room with four bottles of Madeira wine for the examining board. The story is told that much wine was enjoyed, few questions were asked, and he left with his certificate to practice law.³ It was his assignment to pursue his mission in life, and favor was granted to prepare him for the task.

In 1816, Stevens opened his law office in Gettysburg, Pennsylvania. He knew no one in that city, but he soon gained popularity. He invested in real estate with the profits from his practice. In a short time, he became the largest landowner in the community, with interest in some iron furnaces on the outskirts of town. He became involved in politics and served six one-year terms on the borough council between 1822 and 1831. During his early years in Gettysburg, Stevens worked to advance the cause of universal education. During this time, many believed education should be for the wealthy only, excluding children who were impoverished as well as children of color. Stevens believed education should be the tax-free right of each child, black or white and rich or poor.

Stevens's views on education were very similar to Daniel Webster's. "Education, to accomplish the ends of good government, should be universally diffused," Webster said. "Open the door of the schoolhouses to all the children in the land. Let no man have the excuse of poverty for not educating his offspring. Place the means of education within his reach and if he remains in ignorance, be it his own reproach . . . On the diffusion of education among the people rests the preservation and perpetuation of our free institution."⁴ This philosophy centered on the rights of all to develop their gifts and talents in order to become productive citizens and responsible human beings.

Purpose

Stevens was drawn to a path where he could clearly identify his purpose and his assignment. He was concerned with addressing the needs of the poor and downtrodden. He became increasingly aware of the need to develop his voice to uplift humanity. In September of 1833, Stevens was elected to a one-year term in the Pennsylvania legislature.

Stevens worked with Pennsylvania Governor George Wolf in April of 1834 to guide an act through the legislature to provide free public schools in their state. The Gettysburg district voted in favor of this, as well as electing Stevens as a school director. He served in this position until 1839. He made speeches to rally support for public schools as well as for taxes to pay for them. This same act later faced opposition when thousands rallied to repeal it. Despite opposition from Stevens, the request for repeal passed the Senate. But Stevens did not give up the fight, because he knew it was the responsibility of the state government to ensure the availability of a free education for all children.

With his usual skill, Stevens presented his case in Pennsylvania. He believed opponents were seeking to alienate the poor into a lower caste than themselves. He accused the rich of greed and failure to empathize with the poor.

I imagine Christ would have agreed with Stevens and said, "Suffer these children to develop their gifts, skills, and talents, too." Stevens's speech reverberated in the legislative hall. His work toward the cause, along with his influence with Governor Wolf, prevented the bill from being repealed. The Free Public Schools Act enacted in 1834, made Pennsylvania the first state in the nation to provide for a public education system. (hourglassfoundation.org).

Stevens continued on his path. He was now emerging into his life's mission. He had his eyes set on the U.S. House of Representatives. There, he would be able to lift his voice against the institution of slavery in America. He moved his home and law practice to Lancaster, Pennsylvania.[5] As a result of his relocation, he made a memorable friendship with Lydia Hamilton Smith, a mulatto he employed as his housekeeper, and she remained in his service until his death. She was his life companion until he passed away.[6]

Mission

The door to his mission opened in 1848, when he successfully ran to represent the Eighth Congressional District. When Congress convened in December of 1849, Stevens joined other newly elected opponents of slavery, including Salmon P. Chase.[7] This third cobblestone on his pathway enabled him to fight to achieve his life's mission of abolishing slavery in America. He met his colleague for life in the person of Senator Charles Sumner. The congressman and the senator bonded through their resolve to abolish slavery. Absolutely nothing could deter them from their God-given mission. They worked tirelessly to this end. The two men fought the good fight to the close of their lives. Both lived to see the goal of freedom realized with the passage of the Thirteenth Amendment, which abolished slavery in America in 1865.

Courage

God calls his workers to be courageous. Before assigning Joshua to continue the work of Moses guiding the Israelites to the Promised Land, God challenged Joshua to be strong and of good courage. "Have not I commanded thee? Be strong and of a good courage; be not afraid, neither be thou dismayed: for the LORD thy God is with thee whithersoever thou goest" [Josh. 1:9]. Stevens internalized this concept of courage and lived his life unafraid. He did not let the taunting of classmates stop him. He did not let the law examination board stop him. He knew when to change his geographical locations to better serve his work. It took courage to fight for public education for all children in Pennsylvania, and he stayed strong throughout his life.

Obstacles

Stevens did not receive an ordinary assignment. He had to master cobblestone after cobblestone to tread the pathway dictated by his purpose and assignment, staying the course until the completion of his mission. He was born with a clubfoot, his father deserted the family, and his mother assumed both roles to procure a quality education for her sons. Many organizations of his day were biased toward people with physical conditions, but he did not permit any diversions from his path. Stevens persevered through the many challenges to help abolish slavery in America.

Divine Connection

Who gives one the courage, the stamina, the strength, the wisdom, the heart, the mind, and the soul to identify one's purpose in life? Who directs one to the assignment and equips one with the gifts and talents to pursue the mission until the close of life? *Thaddeus Stevens had a divine connection with the Lord, who was his enabler.*

Stevens recognized his assignment early in his life. Early experiences left him with an awareness of his purpose and his gifts. This helped him, in turn, to understand his calling. He pursued a legal career and used his gifts and talents to uplift humanity. Stevens suffered through unique experiences as one who was born with a clubfoot. He endured taunts from classmates and later experienced exclusion from various social venues. Those incidents shaped his attitude and personality, and he embraced his mission—an assignment he took on with heartfelt concern for humankind, God's creation.

Faith

Faith is confidence in God and his humanity. *Faith is the belief that God has created his earth for all humanity.* Faith is the gift of one human sharing with another, knowing that God is the giver to all. Faith is sharing. It is caring for humanity and working toward peace for all who live in God's world. Stevens had faith to guide him in identifying his purpose, developing his gifts, accepting his assignment, and working on his mission until the end of his life before he returned to the Maker who had given him his purpose, assignment, and mission.

Talents

He was an orator, an abolitionist, a teacher, a lawyer, and a realtor. There was great beauty in the way he put his heart into the sharing of his talents to help others realize their own purposes in life. He had earned money from some investments, but he was not profligate. He used his wealth to benefit others. In one instance, he donated land for converting a school into a college. In another, he is said to have provided for the building of an underground tunnel on one of his properties to hide slaves as they traveled toward freedom.

Summary

Thaddeus Stevens was born with a clubfoot but would not let this physical challenge deter him from realizing his *purpose, mission,* and *assignment.* The strong will of his mother to provide the best education possible for her four sons, despite desertion by her husband, made all the difference in his life. He never considered his clubfoot to be an insurmountable physical challenge. He surveyed his gifts to identify his purpose and worked assiduously to accomplish his career goals. As he lifted himself up, he used his gifts to lift up others. *He chose to become a successful lawyer and by doing so, he became equipped to address some of the ills that affected humanity.* He wanted all children to have access to public education. He wanted slaves to become a free people. He followed his career path all the way to the halls of Congress.

Stevens was sworn in as a representative from the state of Pennsylvania in 1849. He remained in those legislative halls, where he fought for this cause until the Thirteenth Amendment was passed in 1865, abolishing slavery in the United States of America. The children of Israel were slaves in Egypt for 430 years. "And the children of Israel did according to the word of Moses; and they borrowed of the Egyptians jewels of sliver, and jewels of gold, and raiment" (Exod. 12:35). As if remembering this biblical reparation, Stevens put forth a resolution to compensate the newly freed slaves. "Forty acres and a mule" refers to the desire of radical Republicans such as Stevens to carry out land redistribution in the South. He wanted to subdivide confiscated land and distribute it among the freedmen. Proposals such as this one failed in Congress and state legislatures. The Slave Codes prevented slaves from being educated and now they were set on the road to freedom without education and without compensation. They had worked as a free labor force to

America for more than two hundred years. Luke 10:7 says clearly that "the laborer is worthy of his hire." The open question remains, "Why did the Congress refused to enact legislation in Congress to provide reparation to this slave population in America? This question still rests before God for an answer.

Ironically, land was available and could have been distributed to the ex-slaves in compensation for their years as a free labor force in the United States. The Homestead Act was passed during the Civil War in 1862. This act provided that "any adult citizen, or intended citizen, who had never borne arms against the U.S. government could claim 160 acres of surveyed government land. After five years on the land, the original filer was entitled to the property, free and clear, except for a small registration fee. Title could also be acquired after only a six-month residency and trivial improvements, provided the claimant paid the government $1.25 per acre. After the Civil War, Union soldiers could deduct the time they had served from the residency requirements." [ourdocuments.gov]

[Information excerpted from Teaching with Documents Using Primary Sources from the National Archives. [Washington, D.C.: National Archives and Records Administration, 1998], p. 31. And from Milestone Documents [Washington, DC: The National Archives and Records Administration, 1995] pp 56-56.)

Thaddeus Stevens's heart was nurtured by the spirit of his mother, who imbued in him a sense of right and wrong and a desire to uplift humanity. He saw the Southern states as conquered provinces after the Civil War and wanted the former slaves to have better lives. He proposed the Fourteenth Amendment, guaranteeing civil rights, and played a leading role in the impeachment of President Andrew Johnson.[8]

Stevens completed his life on August 11, 1868. When his doctor said the end was near, his longtime housekeeper and companion along with his nephews and friends gathered to be with him. Two black preachers prayed with him, telling him that he was in the prayers of all their people. *The New York Times* noted Stevens had "discerned the expediency of emancipation, and urged it long before Mr. Lincoln issued his proclamation."[9]

Stevens's body was taken from his house to the Capitol. Some pallbearers were white and others were former slaves. Thousands of mourners of both races filed past his casket as he lay in state in the rotunda. Stevens was the third man, after Henry Clay and Abraham Lincoln, to receive the honor of having his body viewed in that location. African American soldiers made up the guard of honor. After the service, his body was taken by funeral train to Lancaster, Pennsylvania, a city draped in black for the funeral. There were more than twenty thousand in attendance and half were African Americans.[10]

The inscription on his grave, written by Stevens himself, read as follows:

> I repose in this quiet and secluded spot
> Not from any natural preferences for solitude
> But, finding other Cemeteries limited as to Race
> by Charter Rules
> I have chosen this that I might illustrate in my death
> The Principles which I advocated through a long life;
> *Equality of Man before His Creator.*[11]

His purpose identified, his assignment embraced, and his mission fulfilled, Stevens was laid to rest in Shreiner Cemetery, where people of all races could be buried.

CHAPTER 6

CHARLES SUMNER

Abolishing Slavery In America

Theme: Abolishing slavery from the American nation
Place: Boston, Massachusetts to Washington, D.C.
Born: January 6, 1811
Died: March 11, 1874
Time: Post-American-Revolution, Pre-Civil-War Era

Purpose
Charles Sumner's family life played a very important role in helping him identify his gifts and find ways to fulfill his purpose in life. His father was vehemently against the institution of slavery. As a lawyer, the elder Sumner used many of his gifts to address this situation in the nation. Morality, he believed, was as important for governments as it was for individuals. He felt that there was inherent evil in legal institutions, such as slavery and segregation, that inhibited one's ability to grow. Young Charles had a great opportunity to observe his father working to uplift humanity. He, too, would use his gifts and talents to make a positive impact on the nation. He graduated from Harvard Law School in 1834 and became a protégé of Joseph Story.[1]

In 1837, Charles began his travels in Europe, where he mastered French in six months. He attended lectures on various subjects, such as music, Greek history, and civil law. While pursuing these studies, a most powerful truth was revealed to him as he observed black scholars mingling with other students. "They were standing in the midst of a knot of young men and their color seemed to be no objection to them," he wrote. "I was glad to see this, though with American impressions, it seemed very strange. It must be then that the difference between free blacks and whites among us is derived from education, and does not exist in the nature of things."[2]

He noticed how "the French had no problem with blacks learning and interacting with others." This understanding gave Sumner a new resolve. He would become an abolitionist.

Sumner's three-year stay in Europe gave him the opportunity to study medicine in the city's hospitals, become fluent in Spanish, German, and Italian, and meet many leading statesmen. In 1840, he returned to the United States.

Assignment

Sumner returned to Boston in 1840 at the age of twenty-nine to practice law. The lean, trim six-foot-four-inch man was well versed in many disciplines. He expanded his work to include lecturing at Harvard Law School, editing court reports, and contributing to law journals. His writings included works with historical and biographical themes. He broadened his social relationships to include persons from all walks of life. Henry Wadsworth Longfellow was among the writers, speakers, and poets in his circle. As a gifted orator, he stayed busy on the lecture circuit, speaking on politics, history, and themes from the Bible. Sumner spent much time in heartfelt thought about his mission in life. His travels in Europe had opened his eyes to the way that an education or lack of one could impact a person's life. This revelation pointed to his mission—working with organizations to abolish slavery.[3]

Mission

Sumner, like Stevens, developed his gifts and chose a career assignment in law. His journey was gradually preparing him for his life's mission. In 1851, the door to his mission opened. He took his seat as a US Senator from Massachusetts. The first year was largely a learning experience, but on August 26, 1852, Sumner delivered his first major speech, despite strenuous efforts to dissuade him. The Fugitive Slave Act of 1850 was legislation to address the issue of runaway slaves. Southern plantation owners viewed slaves as their property. When a slave ran away, a Southern planter counted it as property loss. The Fugitive Slave Law stated that runaway slaves were to be returned to their masters. Many northerners objected to this idea and to the new law. Some historians see this legislation as another stone that paved the pathway to the Civil War.

Sumner's first major speech was an attack on the Fugitive Slave Act, the most controversial legislation of the century. The North and the South were becoming more divided over the issue of slavery.[4] Earlier, the issue of slavery had threatened to break up the Constitutional Convention in 1787 before The Great Compromise resolved questions about the allocation of delegates to Congress. It was decided then that three fifths of the slave population would be counted for purposes of representation.

This was a gigantic concern because it was political in nature. The South, with its slave population, wielded more political power than the North and held this status until 1861.[5]

Courage

The Virginia House of Burgesses institutionalized slavery in 1661. The thirteen colonies won their independence, as formally recognized by England in 1783, but failed to ensure liberty for all people. The failure to do so left a shadow upon the land that would haunt the nation until the time of the Civil War. Leaders even ignored Abigail Adams' wisdom and warnings regarding freedom. She had criticized her fellow colonists with these profound words in 1774: "It always appeared a most iniquitous scheme to me to fight ourselves for what we are daily robbing and plundering from those who have as good a right to freedom as we have."[6]

Charles Sumner showed great courage in pursuing his mission—the fight to eradicate slavery across the United States of America.

Sumner's "Crime Against Kansas" speech on May 20, 1856, provoked Congressman Preston Brooks to brutally attack him with a cane. The Crime Against Kansas speech was two-fold in nature. Sumner argued in favor of admitting Kansas into the union as a free state and denouncing Slave Power, which was the political arm of the slave owners, whose goal was to spread slavery throughout the new territories who were seeking admission into the United States.

The unmerciful beating left Sumner close to death. It took three and a half years of respite and a trip to Europe with medical doctors to restore his health. Sumner was able to return to Congress in 1859. He would let nothing prevent him from completing his mission. Brooks was reelected and received hundreds of canes in support of his vile act, but he died January 27, 1857, before he could begin his new term of office.[7]

When some senators tried to come to Sumner's rescue, another southerner, Rep. Laurence Keitt, held a gun and said, "Let it be."[8] When Sumner returned to the Senate in 1859 after his recuperation, he resumed his oratory against slavery. A fire for the cause of freedom was still burning in his soul. He said, "When crime and criminals are thrust before us, they are to be met by all the energies that God has given us by argument, scorn, sarcasm and denunciation."[9] On June 4, 1860, during the presidential election, Sumner delivered another speech, "The Barbarism of Slavery." In it, he depicted slavery as a malevolent institution. He said it had stifled economic development in the South, leaving slaveholders reliant on "the bludgeon, the revolver, and the bowie-knife." This situation was prevalent throughout the South, and large numbers within the poor white population were left unemployed.

Sumner enhanced his oratory with poetic language to accentuate a poignant truth about freedom and humanity. "Say, sir, in your madness, that you own the sun, the stars, the moon; but do not say that you own a man, endowed with a soul that shall live immortal, when sun and moon and stars have passed away."[10] This was reminiscent of the language Thomas Jefferson had used to decry slavery in the first draft of the Declaration of Independence: "He has waged cruel war against human nature itself, violating its most sacred rights of life and liberty in the persons of a distant people who never offended him, captivating and carrying them into slavery in another hemisphere, or to incur miserable death in their transportation thither."[11]

As Chairman of the Foreign Relations Committee, Sumner recognized the economic relationship England and France had with the Confederacy. Some historians believe the South expected these countries to come to their aid during the Civil War. The South was engaged in bustling economic trade with England, exporting cotton, tobacco, and other products. England depended on the cotton for the production of cloth that was sold to her colonies in India. The South believed some European countries would come to its aid for economic reasons. However, Sumner played a vital role in preventing this alliance from becoming a reality and potentially escalating the war. Sumner remained faithful to the cause of freedom for all humanity. This fight was his assignment, and he did not let anything prevent him from fulfilling his mission.

Gifts and Talents

Sumner was a lawyer, a powerful orator, and a gifted essayist. He was the leader of the anti-slavery forces in Massachusetts and the Radical Republicans in the U.S. Senate during the Civil War. Sumner's speech of May 19 and 20, 1856, gives historians a glimpse of how deeply the issue of slavery gripped the nation. Half the country favored freedom, and the other half wanted to spread slavery throughout the union. Sumner spoke vehemently against the expansion of slavery in the nation. The ultimate goal, he thought, was to eradicate this evil from all territories of the United States.

Summary

Charles Sumner can be compared to John the Baptist. He fully engaged his mind, body, and spirit to complete his earthly assignment.

He is to be remembered for his unshakeable moral compass in regard to the sin of slavery. He believed morality was needed in the operations of the government. Without it, he believed, some individuals would go without the opportunity to develop their abilities and the capacity to grow. He held that both slavery and segregation were evil.[12]

Sumner was a man with a great mission. When we review his last words, the heart of the man is revealed. The mortally ill senator said his only regret about dying was he had not finished preparing his collected writings for publication and that the Senate had not yet passed his Civil Rights Bill, which would enforce and protect the civil and legal rights of all citizens. It would give the newly freed slaves equal treatment in matters of public accommodations and public transportation and would prohibit their exclusion from jury service. This bill would later be passed by the 43rd United States Congress and signed into law by President Ulysses S. Grant on March 1, 1875.

Sumner died on the afternoon of March 11, 1874, while still in office. He was 63. Not since the death of Abraham Lincoln in 1865 had the nation grieved so deeply at the loss of one of its statesmen.[13] The country had lost its leading proponent of Reconstruction in the aftermath of the Civil War.

Charles Sumner and Thaddeus Stevens fought vehemently to eradicate slavery in the nation and were the leaders of Radical Reconstruction.[14] They inspired Congress to write legislation to provide freedom, justice, and equality for the newly freed slaves. Stevens wanted each former slave to be compensated with "40 acres and a mule."[15] Both Sumner and Stevens dedicated their lives to make America, in truth, the land of the free and the home of the brave.

CHAPTER 7

Booker T. Washington

Educating Former Slaves to Equip Them for a New Life

Theme: Removing the veil of ignorance from the eyes of American ex-slaves
Place: Virginia, West Virginia, and Alabama
Time: Pre-Civil War days to the nineteenth century
Born: April 5, 1856, on a plantation in Franklin County, Virginia
Died: November 14, 1915, in Tuskegee, Alabama

Purpose

The mission of Booker T. Washington was to lift the veil of ignorance from his people during the post-slavery era. He was born to Jane, a slave. His father was an unknown white man, as was often the case between 1661 and 1865. Jane wanted so much for her children to be free. She prayed constantly for the day when deliverance for all slaves would become a reality.

One day in his childhood, Washington and all the slaves were jubilant when the sound of the freedom bell was heard across the plantation. The slaves were called together to hear the reading of the Emancipation Proclamation and the Thirteenth Amendment, which declared freedom for all.

DR. BOOKER T. WASHINGTON
FOUNDER — TUSKEGEE INSTITUTE

Courtesy of Hampton University Archives

BELIEVE that any man's life will be filled with constant and unexpected encouragements if he makes up his mind to do his level best each day of his life—that is, tries to make each day reach as nearly as possible the highest mark of pure, unselfish, useful living.

Jane gathered her three children and her belongings and began the 400-mile walk on freedom road. Her husband was waiting for their arrival in Malden, West Virginia. Most of the slaves found work in Lewis Ruffner's salt mines. Washington, too, found work as a salt packer, but never lost sight of his goal to acquire an education.

Soon, Washington was transferred to the household of the owner. There, he did domestic work for the owner's wife, Viola Ruffner. He learned everything he could and shared his dreams of achieving an education. He believed within himself that he had a great reason to attend school. Washington was on the pathway to assessing his gifts and was beginning to ascertain his purpose in life.

One day while in the salt mine, he overhead a group of men talking about a school for blacks located in Hampton, Virginia. He wasted no time sharing with his employer his desire to attend the school. She wished him well in his attempt to find it. He walked for miles, thumbed rides, and even rode freight trains and slept underneath doorsteps. Finally, he arrived at Hampton. He was disheveled, unkempt, and muddy-faced from his journey. He knew his priorities. He was more concerned about being admitted than about his appearance. When Miss Mackie, the admission director looked at him, her first thought was to send him away, but instead she decided to give him the administrative test. Washington was assigned to clean a classroom. He had been taught domestic skills by Mrs. Ruffner in West Virginia and was thorough with his work. Later, Miss Mackie, the director, returned with a white handkerchief, which she used to check every desk and chair in the room. When she could not find one particle of dust on her hankie, Washington sighed with relief. He had passed the test and was admitted to this beautiful school.

The prize at the end of the long, rugged trip to Hampton proved to be worth every mile of the journey. Washington envisioned a life spent helping to uplift his people. Education, in his view, was not for social status. It was *an opportunity to light the path for others to follow*. He wanted to help as many people as possible to get an education. Washington now had a schedule of classes and was able to work to pay for his tuition, room, and board.

Assignment

Soon, he was introduced to General Samuel Armstrong, president and founder of Hampton Institute. Armstrong had served as commander of a black military unit during the Civil War. He understood the hardships faced by the former slaves and came up with a plan for Hampton Institute to become a school for them in 1868. Armstrong designed a two-fold curriculum to address the needs of freedmen. While being trained as farmers, carpenters, and bricklayers, they would also learn the value of being sober, hardworking citizens, equipped with skills for employment and land development.

As Washington mastered his studies, he envisioned a life of helping to uplift his people. He wanted to help as many people as possible get educated. In 1875, he graduated from Hampton Institute and took an assignment in West Virginia, teaching children during the day and teaching adults in the evening. He was overjoyed with his accomplishments and found himself sharing his story with anyone who would listen. In this way, he became a recruiter, convincing his girlfriend, Fannie N. Smith, and his brother, James, to also graduate from Hampton Institute.

Mission

After a few years, Armstrong invited Washington back to Hampton Institute to teach sixty students in his Indian program. Washington reflected upon the way his gifts had come to define his purpose. He knew he was called to be an educator, and he enjoyed this work.

Shortly after Washington accepted this position, Armstrong received a request from two gentlemen in Tuskegee, Alabama, who wanted help in finding a principal for their school. Armstrong's response was this: "I have no white man, but I have an excellent black man." The men responded, "Send him right away." Washington was the only person

Armstrong recommended for the Tuskegee school. This opportunity opened the door for Washington to begin his life's work. This assignment was the beginning of his mission—to build a school to teach freedmen to survive from scratch.

Courtesy of Calvin Austin, a Tuskegee graduate

Courage and Overcoming Obstacles

Like Abraham of the Bible, Washington courageously traveled to an unfamiliar place to begin his life's mission. He thought he had been called to become principal of a school, but when he arrived in Tuskegee, he found instead a dilapidated Methodist church with a leaky roof. He took courage, rolled up his sleeves, and canvassed the rural community, finding much to cry about. He knew the Southland was experiencing a grave period as restoration got underway in the post-Civil-War years, but he had to find success in this new assignment. Eliciting help from everyone, he turned down no gifts, gladly accepting, for example, a half dozen eggs from a female octogenarian. After all, it was not the gift but the giver's heart that made all the difference. With faith and courage, Washington kept his focus on his educational mission and vowed to work until his days were done. No task was deemed too difficult and no work too hard as he traveled the path to complete his mission and obtain his goal in life.

Gifts and Talents

Washington was a gifted orator. In 1895, he spoke at the Cotton Exposition in Atlanta, Georgia. The invitation extended to him was a source of worry for some whites. Many were concerned about what he would say, but in essence, he calmed the fears of Southerners with this speech. "In all things that are purely social," he said, "we can be as separate as the fingers, yet one as the hand in all things essential to mutual progress." Frederick Douglass, another great orator, who had worked tirelessly with the abolitionists for so many years, had died on February 20, 1895. Now there was a new black man to lend his voice to the cause. This address, in which he encouraged each listener to "cast down your bucket where you are," became the speech of the century and positioned Washington as a leader of black people across the nation. No leader would address any issue related to blacks without consultation with Washington. This angered some other blacks, such as W.E.B. Dubois and Monroe Trotter—radical men who wanted total equality in all areas. Dubois asked, "If we are not fighting for total equality, in God's name, what are we fighting for?" He had his followers, but the reins of black leadership had been thrust upon Booker T. Washington. President Theodore Roosevelt invited him to dine at the White House, and later, President William Howard Taft and others paid tribute to him by visiting the Tuskegee campus.

Divine Connection

When Samuel Armstrong and Washington met, it was as if they had been brought together by destiny. They were not strangers. It was as if they were meant to work together for a specific purpose to achieve a necessary goal. The relationship from beginning to end was one of father and son. The president played a key role in providing opportunities for growth in the life of Washington. He established a program for him at Hampton Institute and provided a way for him to work to pay for his room and tuition. Armstrong kept communications open with Washington, even when geographical distance separated the two men.

Armstrong recommended Washington for the role of principal of a school, but upon arrival, Washington soon learned there was no school, just a church in disrepair. Washington did not lose faith when he realized there was no school. He used his ingenuity to stay the course and build a school, overseeing the creation of the school's foundation as well as taking care of staffing, recruiting, fundraising, and other areas of need. Washington wanted to acquire as much education as possible. Upon graduating from Hampton, he explored two other careers. He recognized his oratory gifts and sought to apply them in promoting business products. As he sat alone during his personal time, he also pondered the ministry. He found himself enrolled in the Wayland Seminary, located in Washington, D.C.[1] Faith was the guiding light in Washington's work to design Tuskegee Institute.[2]

Washington chose neither a ministry career nor a career in business but found his assignment in education. As founder and president of Tuskegee, however, he employed both his ministry and theological talents as he wrote the curriculum. He used the knowledge he had gained in seminary to integrate moral values into the school's program. He wanted to focus on teaching his people to manage their finances. To this end, he founded the National Negro Business League (NNBL).

Washington was a greater thinker and is often described as a man ahead of his time. He was constantly thinking of ways to uplift his brethren—the ex-slaves. He was able to observe them in their natural environment and wanted to create opportunities for them to grow, to build better lives, and to become self-sufficient. He thought of a new way to teach his people to manage and increase their finances. This culminated in his plan to form the National Negro Business League. *His idea became reality in Boston, Massachusetts, in 1900, preceding the United States Chamber of Commerce by twelve years.* His goal was to bring commercial and economic prosperity to the African American community. A model was created and chapters formed across the United States. The National Negro Business League was reincorporated in 1966 in Washington, DC.[3]

Washington wanted to teach the former slaves to manage their households well and build their communities with pride. The NNBL was made up of small business owners, farmers, doctors, lawyers, craftsmen, and other professionals. Our community, during my growth years, was Washington's vision come to life. In our community, blacks owned a variety of businesses, including a satellite post office, medical office, shoe shop, barber shop, drug stores, food stores, cafes, and social clubs. We had choices when it came to careers.

Faith

Washington's goals would not have been realized if he had not walked in faith as he undertook his journey. When the freedom bell rang in 1865, Washington and his family put their feet on the freedom path to West Virginia. He had no idea he would hear the greatest news of his life in a salt mine, but he walked by faith. He overheard two men talking about a school for blacks, and acting in faith, he found the school and realized his dream of obtaining an education. In faith, he took a job teaching in West Virginia, but he had no idea this would be a time of preparation for his life assignment. He encouraged his brother and girlfriend to attend Hampton Institute, and they later found employment at Tuskegee. Faith is the spiritual gift of believing and not walking by sight. Throughout his life, Washington walked by faith and not by sight.

Walking by Faith: A Story Worth Telling

Booker T. Washington's prize at the end of the long, rugged trip to Hampton, Virginia, was worth every mile of the journey. Upon admission to Hampton Institute, he wanted to avail himself to as many opportunities as possible. He took advantage of a variety of educational programs. He was slowly developing his philosophy of life. Education, in his view, was not for social status; it was an opportunity to light the path for others to follow. He wanted to help as many people as possible to acquire an education. In 1875, Washington graduated from Hampton. He returned home to take an assignment in West Virginia, teaching children during the day, and teaching adults in the evening program. He was so overjoyed with his assignment that he shared his story with anyone who would listen and recruited others to the program.

Armstrong invited Washington to return to Hampton to teach sixty students in his Indian program. Washington had identified his gifts, defined his purpose, and prepared himself for his assignment. He knew he was called to be an educator, and he enjoyed this work.

Finally, Armstrong turned on the light that guided Washington on the trail toward accomplishing his mission. Armstrong said to Washington that he had a letter from two gentlemen in Alabama requesting a principal for their school. The request was for a white man, but Armstrong had replied that he had a black man who was excellent. Armstrong received an immediate response from the gentlemen: he was to send the black man right away.

By Faith, Not by Sight

Oftentimes, one has to have tenacity and persistence to accomplish his or her mission. Moses, in his mission to free the Israelites from Pharaoh's bondage, learned the group would have to make bricks without straw. When Washington arrived at Tuskegee, he found no school, just a church in great need of repair. Instead of giving up and returning to Virginia, Washington rolled up his sleeves and canvassed the rural community for support in making this school a reality. He smiled, in gratitude, when a female octogenarian walked in to offer her half dozen eggs as a donation to the building of the school.

Making bricks without straw was his reality, he had to design a curriculum, recruit teachers and students, in addition to performing a variety of tasks to bring his school to life. In truth, he had to be a "jack of all trades." When finances became a major problem, he called on Armstrong, who had become a surrogate father to him. The Tuskegee school was of a similar design to that of Hampton Institute. Those who had known and worked with Washington were proud of his work and assisted him in his progress whenever possible. Washington built the school and purchased more land until he had expanded Tuskegee beyond his imagination. The school's curriculum addressed the needs of the newly freed slaves, instilling in them a moral code and equipping them with skills. When students reported for admission, they blushed with chagrin to know each individual had to show his or her personal toothbrush. Proper hygiene was a priority—there would be no sharing of the tooth brush. Washington had survived the shackles and hardships of slavery. He was cognizant of the needs of the students and set as his goal to nurture total development.

When Washington delivered his "Atlanta Compromise" speech in 1895, he changed the trajectory of the lives of blacks across the nation. Overnight he became a national figure, with invitations pouring in from those who wanted him to speak. In addition, money came in from philanthropists for his Institute.[4]

What was the campus like in 1895? It had 800 students, 55 staff members, buildings valued at $200,000, and 165 graduates. Enrollment figures grew after the famous speech, and donations made it possible for new buildings to be erected on the campus. These included Dorothy Hall, Douglas Hall, Institute Chapel, and more.[5]

The growth at Tuskegee spiraled onward and upward. The results were more than sixty buildings and an endowment of nearly $3 million dollars by 1915. Now internationally famous, Washington never slowed his pace until his death on November 14, 1915. He had used his gifts to identify his purpose, prepared himself for his assignment, and completed his mission.[6]

On November 12, 1915, a train carried a gravely ill Washington to Tuskegee from a hospital in New York City. He had often said he wanted to end his days in the region of his birth. Two days later, he slipped into a coma and passed away four hours after his arrival. "I was born in the South," he once said. "I have lived in the South, and I expect to die and be buried in the South."[7]

Comparative Views on Education

Thaddeus Stevens and the governor of Pennsylvania had led the fight for free public schools in their times, other congressmen continued in the quest to provide great educational opportunities. Stevens was appalled at how the wealthy were concerned only for the education of their own children, therefore, he used his oratorical, legal, and political skills to ensure that all children would have access to free education. Mindful of the education he had been given, he wanted these children to have the opportunity to develop the gifts God had given them at birth. His mother had moved from town to town to make sure a quality education would be available to him. He fought to make that kind of education a reality for poor children and black children. He believed all children should have the opportunity to develop their gifts in order to make a positive difference and uplift humanity.

Senator Hubert Humphrey and other legislators helped pass laws during the 1960s to provide opportunities for students to attend college with remunerations. John F. Kennedy introduced the Peace Corps to broaden the minds of youth as they cared for humanity across the globe. After completing a two-year assignment, these students' graduate education was financed by the government. There were no corporations exploiting youth with high-interest-bearing loans. These leaders took to heart the directive in the preamble to the Constitution to care for "our posterity." They were of the mindset that it was the responsibility of the nation to teach, train, and develop the nation's children to pave the way for a stronger and brighter tomorrow and to provide high-power job opportunities to the nation's posterity, not to provide hidden agendas for corporate exploitation. The land of the free is that banner that should sing a note of praise for up and coming Americans with love, hope, and justice.

The U.S. Congress was packed in the 1960s with senators and representatives who had love and compassion for the nation's children. Following the lead of those who had set out to "ordain and establish this Constitution for ourselves and our posterity," these leaders continued to take responsibility to light the way for future generations. I was able to attend college because these responsible legislators enacted laws to strengthen the nation through investments in education for the children of the nation. The Education Act for Elementary and Secondary schools had been passed by Congress to help make college education more affordable.

GENERAL SAMUEL C. ARMSTRONG IS LOCATED IN THE
WINDOW ON THE LEFT SIDE. BOOKER T. WASHINGTON IS
LOCATED ON THE RIGHT SIDE OF THE BRICK WALL.

Courtesy of Hampton University Archives

Summary

Under the divine guidance of the Lord, Booker T. Washington worked to design and develop a school for blacks to prepare them to improve their lives in post-slavery America. He built an institution to equip them with skills in bricklaying, millinery, lumbering, farming, and carpentry work. The school instilled in them a sense of morality and a drive to work together to build a positive community and transmit this way of life to the next generation. Booker T. Washington identified his talents, understood his purpose, embraced his assignment, and remained faithful to his mission in life until his days were done.

A Graduate's Testimony to the Continuing
Legacy of Booker T. Washington

As a student at Tuskegee, I had the great opportunity to benefit from the philosophy of Washington's institute turned university. I am most appreciative of the moral teachings infused into the curriculum. There was the family atmosphere, the Sunday chapel services with required attendance, and various work-opportunity programs.

The philosophy of Tuskegee was to embrace the student body as a family, nurture, and guide them to succeed in their quest to earn a college degree. The heart and soul of Tuskegee were invested in the members of the staff and faculty who viewed their position as more than a job. They were cognizant of our heritage as a people emerging from bondage. They put their hearts and souls into teaching. Although students may have travelled from various cities throughout Alabama and other locations, the faculty embraced them as family. The faculty members taught their disciplines, but they were also devoted to the mission of developing the total individual. They had the opportunity to write the history of a people who had emerged from slavery. The staff and faculty educated their students in as many ways as possible. They provided services to assist students in identifying and developing their gifts and talents with their hearts set on using them to uplift humanity.

This philosophy, "each one, reach one," created the climate for the Tuskegee family and was in keeping with the great work of Booker T. Washington and George Washington Carver. There were no big "I's" and little "u's." The campus climate radiated with a spirit of camaraderie, as those at Tuskegee sought to assist each individual to realize his or her dream. Graduates were sent out into the world with instructions to share this gift of inspiration with as many people as possible. The faculty and staff stood ready to extend a helping hand to a hard-working student who was trying to succeed and perhaps, to be a role model for younger siblings.

When I entered Tuskegee, I had to meet with Mr. Davis, the financial aid officer, who dealt with matters regarding tuition and sometimes room and board. I shared my story as my introduction. "I am from Fairfield," I told him. "I am the fifth of twelve, and my dad works in the steel plant. I am the first in my family to go college. My mother remains home to care for the children and household." When I completed my introduction, Mr. Davis spoke. "It is my great pleasure to meet you and to welcome you to Tuskegee. I will do everything in my power to assist you in obtaining your college degree." He was true to his word. I graduated from Tuskegee in a little under four years.

Mr. Davis had accepted my admission application and awarded me a grant for the second semester. I entered during the spring session. Upon completing my first semester, I was able to obtain summer employment in New York to earn money for my room and board. This became my employment pattern for three summers. I had acquired great typing skills in high school, so in my last year at Tuskegee, I was able to secure employment on the campus with Mrs. Freddye Burns in the library cataloguing division, and this employment made all the difference. I earned enough money for my room and board and for enrollment in summer school. Staff members went beyond the call of duty. It was that Booker T. Washington spirit, with each one reaching out to make a difference in an individual's life whenever they recognized a need, much as a family member might do. One semester I did not have enough money to pay for room and board. I was blessed when music professor Mrs. Lexine Weeks invited me to live with her from mid-November to the end of that school year, when I would return to New York for summer employment.

I recall that Mrs. Burns' assistant was about my size and graciously gave me gifts of clothing. We, as aspiring college graduates, rallied under the philosophy of prioritizing and making sacrifices to realize the goal of achieving a college education. I knew my first priority was to save enough money to meet my obligations—paying my room and board. I knew I had to make sacrifices to earn my degree. Later, upon graduation and beginning my employment, I would be able to expand my budget accordingly. I applied this sense of discipline throughout my life. I began teaching in New York, and I wanted to make sure I made payments on my National Defense Education Act loan in time, because I wanted my record to show I was responsible and caring. I wanted this opportunity to be available for other students. When I mailed my first installment to the financial aid officer at Tuskegee, I informed him of my employment. He mailed a receipt and provided me with unknown information: "If you are teaching in a school with a Title I or Title II program which teaches remedial reading and math, you complete this form at the end of each year. After teaching five years in this school, you will receive cancellation of your loan." I was blessed to receive that cancellation. I was thankful to the officer at Tuskegee for sharing that information with me.

I had my goals and I knew my priorities. New York City has an excellent transportation system. Instead of purchasing a car in my first year of employment, I chose to use a portion of my salary to pursue a graduate degree at New York University. This degree qualified me to get paid at the highest salary level. Later, I earned another graduate degree from New York University; this one was in educational administration. As I did my research for this publication, I realized I was truly "a Booker T. Washington student." Washington attended the Wayland Theological Seminary in DC after he graduated from Hampton Institute in 1875. I earned my master of divinity from New York Theological Seminary. I now understand how the founder integrated his theological studies into the curriculum. Freshmen and sophomores were required to attend Sunday chapel services, located then in Logan Hall. Students were permitted three or four cuts without penalty. When I look back across the years, I am most appreciative of the chapel services. The awe-inspiring services presided over by Chaplain Wynn played a vital role in molding and shaping my philosophy for living. There were guest speakers as well as classical and cultural programs integrated into the vesper and chapel services. In the 1970s, students began to protest the requirement to attend the services, wanting attendance to be optional. As we observe now in our culture, we have lost so much understanding about how humans should relate to one another in a way that upholds high morals. When morality is removed, crime, violence, and immorality take their toll. I considered the chapel services to have been a great blessing.

For me, it was truly an honor and a blessing to graduate from Booker T. Washington's Tuskegee Institute. The philosophy of "each one, to reach one" came alive at the school. I was a first-generation college graduate who served as a model for six younger siblings to obtain a college education. As an educator—teacher, counselor, and administrator—I had the opportunity of guiding thousands of children and inspiring them to get college degrees. "A little lump, leavens the whole loaf." As Booker T. Washington was, I, too, was a recruiter for the school. I worked with the Moton College Recruitment program to encourage students from the North to attend historically black colleges and universities (HBCUs). My sons are graduates of the HBCUs.

I meet my students in my travels to various cities. A typical comment goes like this: "Mrs. Swygert, you don't know how many students you have motivated. They are doctors, lawyers, leaders in businesses, educators, and inventors across the nation. We are so thankful we had you as our guidance counselor, not to mention the cultural impact you made on us with your black history and career seminars. We just want you to know we thank you!"

I recall the devoted work of Dr. Toland, who used Dr. John Hope Franklin's text to teach black history and culture. While working in the library, I had the opportunity to meet Dr. Franklin in person. I made a pledge to myself to read the 639-page book *From Slavery to Freedom* from cover to cover after graduation. This provided me with knowledge about the history and culture of African Americans. After my third year of teaching, I was one of forty educators selected to participate in the NDEA (National Defense Educational Act) government sponsored program to train educators nationally to infuse school curriculums with African American history. I worked with curriculum writing in school districts in New York.

UP FROM
SLAVERY
By Booker T. Washington

Courtesy of Hampton University Archives

CHRONOLOGY
OF
BOOKER T. WASHINGTON
Founder of Tuskegee Institute
1856 - 1915

1856   (April 5) Born in Franklin County, Virginia; son of a slave, Jane, and unknown white father.

1865   End of Civil War. Adoption of Thirteenth Amendment abolishing slavery.

1865   Moves with mother and stepfather to Malden, West Virginia.

1865-71   Works in salt mines and coal mines in Malden.

1871-72   Works as houseboy in home of Mrs. Lewis Ruffner [Viola].

1872-75   Attends Hampton Normal and Agricultural Institute, graduating with honors in 1875.

1875-78   Teaches school in Malden.

1877   End of Reconstruction Era in South.

1878-79   Attends Wayland Seminary, Washington, DC.

1879-81   Teaches at Hampton Institute.

1881   Founds and becomes first principal of Tuskegee Institute, Tuskegee, Alabama.

1882   Marries Fannie N. Smith of Malden (d. 1884).

1883   Supreme Court decision in Civil Rights Cases.

1884   Delivers address, "The Educational Outlook in the South," in Madison, Wisconsin before the National Educational Association.

1885   Marries Olivia A. Davidson of Ohio (d. 1889).

1892   First Annual Tuskegee Negro Conference.

1893   Marries Margaret James Murray of Mississippi.

1895   (September 18) Delivers address as Negro representative at opening of *the* Cotton States and International Exposition, Atlanta, Georgia.

1896	Speaks at Harvard University commencement and receives honorary MA degree from Harvard.
1896	Supreme Court decision in Plessy v. Ferguson upholds state segregation law.
1898	(February) Appeals to Louisiana Constitutional Convention on subject of Negro disfranchisement.
1898	(December, 16, 1898) President William McKinley visits Tuskegee.
1899	Visits Europe.
1900	Organizes National Negro Business League.
1901	Publishes *Up From Slavery.*
1901	Receives honorary doctorate from Dartmouth College.
1901	(October) White House Dinner. President Theodore Roosevelt consults with Washington about political appointments in the South.
1902	William Monroe Trotter begins publication of *Boston Guardian*, attacking Washington as race leader.
1903	W.E.B. Du Bois publishes "Of Mr. Booker T. Washington and Others" in *Souls of Black Folk*, publicly criticizing Washington.
1905	Founding of Niagara Movement.
1909	Founding of the National Association for the Advancement of Colored People.
1911	Publishes *My Larger Education.*
1911	Travels in Europe.
1912	Publishes *The Man Farthest Down.*
1915	(November 14) Dies in Tuskegee, Alabama.

Information Source: *Hampton University Archives, Hampton University, Hampton, Virgini*

CHAPTER 8

GEORGE WASHINGTON CARVER

Teaching Farmers and Ex-slaves to Survive After the Civil War

Theme: A gifted American scientist

Place: Missouri, Iowa, Alabama

Time: 1864-1943

Born: 1864—Diamond, Missouri

Died: January 5, 1943

Parents: Moses and Susan Carver (surrogate)

Moses Carver was a German immigrant who had purchased George's parents, Mary and Giles, from William P. McGinnis on October 9, 1855, for approximately $700.

> *You must learn all you can, then go back out into the world and give your learning to your people.*
>
> —Mariah Watkins

Purpose

George Washington Carver was born one year before the end of slavery. He had a brother, James, and a sister. The family was tragically broken apart when night raiders kidnapped George, his mother, and sister. Moses Carver, who had purchased George's parents about nine years earlier, hired John Bentley to try to bring them back.[1] He was unsuccessful in locating everyone but found baby George underneath a tree. He was not expected to live, but Susan Carver nursed him back to health. Health issues continued for Carver throughout his life. He was a frail man of small stature and retained a light, high-pitched voice. Susan took great care of him throughout his childhood and youth. His brother, who escaped being kidnapped, did fieldwork, but Susan had a more delicate assignment for George. Little George was taught domestic work. He learned everything about operating the household. After completing his chores, he was given free time, which he used to roam in nature.

Again, we can assess how childhood experiences can sometimes help a person identify their purpose. Susan's decision to permit George to do domestic work helped him understand what he was meant to do in life. The free time he had after his domestic chores gave him the opportunity to study nature. He carefully studied the plants and flowers in the woods until he knew how to heal and restore dying plants.

He often found joy in lending his services to neighbors. He was affectionately known as the "plant doctor." His love of plants and the joy he found working in nature inspired him to probe deeper and learn more. He wanted to get an education. Unlike the white children, children from the newly freed slave families had few schools available to them. The Locust School was one mile from the Carver home, but it was for white children. Susan and Moses taught George to read, write, and do some arithmetic, using the Webster's old Blue Back Speller, but he wanted to learn more. Finally, at around age twelve, he decided to find a school that black children could attend.

He took courage to search for this school. After walking for ten miles, he found the Lincoln School in Neosho, Missouri. He found another surrogate mother in Mariah Watkins.[22] She took him to her Methodist church and enrolled him in the school for blacks.

Obstacles

Mariah nurtured George as if he were her own son. She introduced him to Stephen Frost, a teacher at the Lincoln School. She guided him in Bible study and taught him to identify more plants and about the uses of these plants. As he performed chores in her home to pay for his room and board, he acquired many skills. Mariah taught him the laundry business and shared her knowledge of black history. Skills learned at her side prepared him to do odd jobs in his travels as he sought to take care of himself and acquire a high school diploma. She taught him the value of self-worth and dignity. When he first met Mariah, Carver introduced himself as "Carver's George." Mariah responded quickly to correct this language: "You are not Carver's George, you are George Carver!" This new way of seeing himself remained with him for life. As they discussed the Bible, Mariah impressed upon his heart the need to know one's purpose in life. "You must learn all you can," she told him, "then go back out into the world and give your learning to your people."

After spending three years at the Lincoln School, George had a burning desire to further his education. When he heard about a couple who was planning to travel west, he saw an opportunity to ride with them to further his search for advanced education. He wanted to earn a high school diploma. He said goodbye to Mariah and traveled with the Smiths, who were relocating to Kansas. He thought he would find a school in this state. He did find a foster-care family, headed by a colored blacksmith in Fort Scott, Kansas, but had a very unfortunate experience. On March 26, 1879, at the age of fifteen, Carver observed a black man being pulled out of jail, strung up, hanged, and later burned. He had never witnessed anything like that in his life, and the memory stayed with him forever.[3] He departed that town the same night!

Despite the various hardships he endured, Carver did not abandon his idea of earning a high school diploma. Finally, he achieved this dream and received his diploma from Minneapolis High School in Kansas.[4] He applied to and was accepted at Highland University in Highland, Kansas, but when school officials realized he was black, he was denied admission. The caustic words, "We do not admit Negroes, never did, and never will," deflated his spirit.[5] He knew God was guiding his steps and opening his mind to his purpose in life, but this painful rejection wounded his soul. He read his Bible to find solace, and the memory of Mariah's words challenged and inspired him. He wanted to give up, but her lessons were embedded deeply within him. He knew he would find the key to unlock the next door to fulfill his mission in life. Carver traveled further west and met some people who introduced him to an opportunity to purchase land. He met some friendly Indians who taught him survival skills. He learned to distinguish poisonous plants from edible ones. Two plants he learned to identify as edible food were the tipsin plant, which is similar to turnip greens, and the mindo plant, which tastes like a sweet potato. He was appreciative of this knowledge as he traveled the western lands. In his travels he also learned of Turkey Red Wheat, which had been introduced by Russian Mennonites. This wheat was unique in its capacity to resist drought.

Courage

Carver's journey was marked by courage. At age twelve, he took courage to walk ten miles to find a school that accepted black students. During his travels out West, he pursued his goal of obtaining a high school education. He would not let disappointments keep him from his goal. Once on his travels, he was confronted by two white men who asked, "Boy, what are you doing with those books?" They came to their own conclusion: "He must have stolen them from some dutiful white person."

Poor George had worked odd jobs to earn money to purchase these books, and now they were taken from him, but he retained that burning desire in his heart to earn a high school diploma, and he would not let anything deprive him of reaching that milestone.

When one is on the path to identifying one's purpose and assignment in life, one has to embrace courage, tenacity, and persistence to reach the goal. Carver persisted! He persisted despite the fact that he had been accepted at Highland College only to appear and hear distressing news: "We do not accept Negroes in this college, never did, and never will." These remarks could have been enough to deter Carver from ever seeking admission to another college, but with his faith in God and his divine connection, windows opened in his life to enable him to begin the mission he had been born to pursue.

THE GEORGE WASHINGTON CARVER MUSEUM, LOCATED ON THE TUSKEGEE UNIVERSITY CAMPUS.

Courtesy of Calvin Austin, a Tuskegee graduate

Mission

Carver's first visit to Tuskegee mirrored Booker T. Washington's first visit to the same place. Washington thought he had received an assignment to be a principal, but when he arrived, he realized he had to design and build a school. When Washington asked Carver to come to Tuskegee, Carver was under the impression that Tuskegee Institute had a science department and a research laboratory. He was accustomed to a full science department with a model farm program, but when he arrived at Tuskegee, he was in for a rude awakening. He, like Booker T. Washington before him, persevered. He had to search dumps to find items essential to his work. He converted discarded items into laboratory equipment. Carver found strength from within, and his faith in God enabled him to overcome struggles to achieve his mission. There was absolutely nothing that would deter him from his journey.

Assignment

Carver graduated from Iowa College and was invited to enter the graduate program to earn his master's degree. He completed this degree in 1896 and was hired in the department. The impossible dream had become a reality. He had used his gifts and talents to prepare himself to take his assignment in life.

Gifts and Talents

As the "Savior of Southern Agriculture," he revolutionized his field. He found more than three hundred uses for the peanut and over a hundred uses for the sweet potato.

Carver developed many techniques to improve soil that had been depleted by repeated cotton plantings. His scientific work in the field of agriculture made an immense difference in the ability of farmers to plant, grow, and rotate crops to enrich the land. When he went to Tuskegee, he began publishing agricultural bulletins to enlighten readers and introduce new methods of planting and growing crops. He promoted environmentalism. He worked to improve the lives of farmers. He had deep a concern for the farmers who lived far out in rural communities with no way to travel in pursuit of learning, so he designed a school on wheels. The Morris Ketchum Jesup Agricultural Wagon carried knowledge to these farmers so they could stay up to date.[6] He also wrote bulletins and distributed them to the rural farmers. Once or twice a year, he invited them to attend his agricultural conferences and to bring samples of the products they had learned to grow. This empowered these farmers to heal their land, to learn, and to better feed their families.

Carver's presence was in great demand by blacks and whites alike. He is often referred to as the "Savior of Southern Agriculture." During the 1920s, the boll weevil from Mexico nearly destroyed agriculture in the South. The boll weevil is a beetle that feeds on cotton buds and flowers. The primary crop in the South was cotton. Throughout the South, cotton was deemed "King," and it was exported to England and other countries in Europe. In the face of the boll weevil threat, Carver introduced scientific methods to save southern agriculture.

In 1941, Time magazine referred to Carver as a "Black Leonardo."[7] He had been confronted with racism in his quest to acquire an education, but, despite the various obstacles placed on his path, he refused to let anything prevent him from achieving his goal of earning a degree. Later in life, he was acknowledged at a science conference. While some scientists shared the various stages of their work, illuminating their discoveries, Carver did the opposite. He acknowledged God as the director and innovator responsible for his achievements. He talked about having dreams that directed him to go out into nature to find specific items. He and Harriet Tubman shared this spiritual gift. It led Carver to make new scientific discoveries and guided Tubman in her work with the Underground Railroad. However, many of Carver's fellow scientists rejected his remarks as being unscientific, but Carver was speaking from personal experience about his relationship with God. He recognized him as the One who had guided his hand. To illustrate his point, he shared with them a memory of working in his laboratory while doing research on the peanut. Carver had recognized the value of the peanut, but others did not perceive it as a good source of human food. Carver said the peanut was not just for animals but could provide nutrition for people as well. He began his work to prove his scientific assessment of the peanut. He locked himself in his laboratory and asked God to reveal to him all the secrets and uses of the peanut. Some of the old guard at Tuskegee love to share stories about the scientist. "When some students would knock on the locked lab door," one professor said, "Carver responded, 'Go away, I am in conversation with God on the peanut!'" Carver set out to discover as many new things as he could— in the woods, in the laboratories, and in conversation with God.

Divine Connections

Carver did have divine connections. He met Dr. John and Helen Milholland, and they made all the difference in his life. John Milholland was born in 1843 in Ohio. He served in the military during the Civil War. He married Helen Frisbie in 1871. After completing his medical degree, he opened a family practice in Winterset, Iowa, in 1882.

In 1888, Carver moved to the same town, where he began working odd jobs and taking in laundry. He began attending a church where Milholland was a leader. Carver joined the choir, and his gift of singing caught the attention of Helen Milholland, prompting her husband to extend a dinner invitation to him. Soon, the Milhollands learned of Carver's college rejection, and they set him on a new path.

Carver finally was admitted to Simpson College in Indianola, Iowa, in 1890. He studied art, and his teacher, Etta Budd, recognized his interest in plants and agriculture.[8] She also knew there were few employment opportunities for blacks in his area of interest. She, therefore, decided to refer Carver to the college where her father was chairman of the Iowa Agricultural College and Model Farm. This connection made all the difference in his life. Carver took his art teacher's advice, and soon he had made the transfer. Etta Budd's father had been delighted to admit him to his college.[9]

The college had a greenhouse and a model farm, and Carver studied horticulture and botany. He was mentored by Professor Louis Pammel, an expert in the field of mycology, which focuses on the genetic, biomedical, and other properties of fungi. Carver had an inquisitive mind, and being admitted to study in this department of the school made all the difference in his life. He embraced as lifelong friends the Milhollands and Etta Budd. The same was true of the bookstore owner Mrs. Arthur Liston, who used her influence to make the campus more welcoming for Carver.

Carver was confronted with some challenges as the first black on this college campus. Upon admission, he learned he was not permitted to eat in the dining hall with the other students. Instead, he had to take his meals in the basement. Friends to whom he corresponded rallied to rectify the college climate for him. Mrs. Liston wasted no time in visiting the campus. She was dressed in finery and carried a charming parasol as Carver escorted her across the campus. She used her influence to introduce him to chairpersons and to students in various classes to ensure his smooth transition to college life. She told them of Carver's gifts, his homesteading in 1882, and his survival of the blizzard of 1888. Mrs. Liston's visit impacted his adjustment to college life.

After her visit and introductions, Carver found himself being integrated into campus life, experiencing a variety of activities, and engaging in various programs. He fascinated the chemistry chairperson with his knowledge of plants and flowers. The students on the campus even convinced Carver to enter his paintings in the World's Fair, which opened to the public on May 1, 1893, in Chicago. The city was illuminated for the first time with Nikola Tesla's game-changing alternating current, which had been chosen over Thomas Edison's direct current to power the exposition. It certainly proved to be a rewarding experience for Carver.

The fair encompassed six hundred acres and more than twenty-seven million people attended.[10]

Carver recognized that a divine connection had been made when Booker T. Washington invited him to Tuskegee Institute. Carver saw this as a way to follow the heartfelt advice of Mariah Watkins: "You must learn all you can, then go back out into the world and give your learning to your people." The two ex-slaves worked for decades to lift the veil of ignorance from the eyes of former slaves after the Civil War, equipping them to use their gifts and talents to not only prosper but to enrich their communities as well.

As he read Washington's letter, Carver heard Mariah's quiet voice urging him to use his learning to enrich the lives of ex-slaves. After reading the letter several times, his heart gave him the answer. He mailed a response to Washington, and told him, "I will come." This decision made Tuskegee Institute one of the most powerful centers of learning for the newly freed slaves. A divine connection had been made! Both Washington and Carver had been born into slavery, and both had earned college degrees before the turn of the century.

Carver also recognized a divine connection when he was admitted to Iowa State College after his rejection from Highland College. Carver embraced the divine connection of his birth, allowing him to be nurtured by his surrogate parents, Moses and Susan Carver. Moses was a German farmer who had benefited from purchasing cheap land under the Preemption Act of 1841 during the presidency of John Tyler. He and his wife were born around 1812 and lived until 1910. The Preemption Act permitted settlers to stake a claim on acreage and, after they had been residents for about fourteen months, buy the property from the government for as little as $1.25 an acre. They could purchase up to 160 acres (65 ha). Moses Carver's 160-acres of land was located in Marion Township in Newton County, Missouri.[11]

Armstrong Hall is located on Tuskegee University campus. Checks saved by George Washington Carver were used to help finance this building.

Courtesy of Calvin Austin, a Tuskegee graduate

Faith

Carver knew God wanted him to fulfill his purpose in life, and he refused to let any disappointments divert him from his path in preparing himself to fulfill his mission. Despite various challenges he faced in trying to obtain an education, he did not let anything or anyone cause detours on his journey. After meeting Mariah Watkins, he embraced the Bible as his guide in life. When disappointments came, such as the rejection from Highland College, he found refuge in the Good Book. He persevered and stayed on his journey until the mission was complete.

Carver had faith in the work God had assigned him. God revealed to Carver the value of the peanut and, as with most of his research findings, Carver shared this knowledge to uplift humanity. Guided by the hand of God, Carver spent many hours in his laboratory researching the value of the peanut.

The United Peanut Association of America invited Carver to give a presentation on the value and uses of the peanut. During the second decade of the twentieth century, China was seeking to import the peanut to America at a price with which American businessmen could not compete. Instead, they petitioned Congress to place a high tariff on Chinese peanut imports. Carver played a crucial role in popularizing the peanut. On January 20, 1921, he made a presentation before the U.S. Congress on the ways the peanut could benefit the American economy. Based on this presentation, Congress enacted a bill to place a tariff on peanut imports.[12]

TOMPKINS DINING HALL ON TUSKEGEE UNIVERSITY CAMPUS

Courtesy of Calvin Austin, a Tuskegee graduate

Stories Shared by Those Who Knew Carver

A Dream: Watermelon and Pocketknife

Carver's experience with dreams echoed those of Joseph in the Bible. Joseph not only had dreams, but he was gifted by God with an ability to interpret them. Carver, like Joseph, found guidance in his dreams. They led him to make discoveries and to do scientific work.

Oftentimes, Carver's dreams directed his behavior. Several times he received dreams when he was engaged in research. Upon awakening, he walked outside on missions of discovery to learn his dreams had led him on the right paths.

As a young boy with great hopes of finding a school for blacks, Carver prayed for a sign to inform him when he should leave home to search for a school. He also wanted to own a personal pocket knife. A pocketknife to Carver was a sign that it would be okay to undertake the journey. As he pondered a possible journey, he dreamt of a watermelon with a pocketknife stuck inside, as if someone had been eating the fruit. When he awakened, he ran down to the field and saw half a watermelon with a pocketknife sticking out. He was no longer puzzled about what to do. He was certain he had received an affirmation. The dream taught him to trust in God. He had received his sign and he knew he could trust God to direct his way as he traveled to locate a school that blacks could attend. He was encouraged to trust God and to begin his journey.

A Very Frugal Man

During my first semester at Tuskegee, I had the honor of being a student in Dr. Otis's consumer economics class. Each class was more interesting than the one before. He loved telling stories about Carver. My mother was a great storyteller too, and she gathered us around her knee to read Bible stories. Both my parents shared stories of their childhoods in rural Alabama. We were fireside children, drinking in wisdom around the fireplace. I became a great reader and a lover of books.

As Dr. Otis admonished his students to become thriftier, he shared stories about Carver and told us there was no one as thrifty as Carver had been. He said Carver did not cash any of his checks. When he died in 1943, there was an accumulation of them that were used to construct a science research center. We knew this as Armstrong Hall. "Carver," the professor said, "would not spend money on his wardrobe. He was a frequent customer at the shoe repair shop. He would patch his shoes over and over again."

When I think of this frugal scientist, my heart swells at the image of the man who had one purpose in life: to complete his assignment and fulfill his mission.

Professor Otis reminisced how Carver was world famous and in great demand as a speaker and a presenter. When waiting on a bench to be picked up at a train station before a presentation, he was often overlooked because of the way he was dressed. Of course, in our times, we would say, "I have to dress to reflect my role and to represent who I am as a person." I am sure Carver would feel a kinship with John the Baptist.

Stay the Course or Surrender!

Dr. Otis shared another story and rooted it in biblical ethics. He held this story close to his heart. It was the story about Carver being turned away from Highland College.

Carver was driven by the Spirit of God to get an education. He worked, courageously, to make this a reality, taking on a variety of odd jobs to obtain his education.

This story is reflective of the various trials an individual may face in seeking to identify one's purpose, realize one's mission, and remain faithful to a God-given assignment.

Carver recognized his interest in studying plants and flowers. As a young lad, he walked ten miles to locate a school in Missouri that would admit black students—the Lincoln School in Neosho. In search of advanced education, he then traveled to Kansas. He had no relatives to take him in, but with courage and faith, Carver made his way through the western territories, worked odd jobs, took in laundry, and performed domestic work until, finally, he graduated from Minneapolis High School in Kansas in 1884.

When one is seeking to realize one's purpose, mission, and assignment [PMA], one has to stay focused. As one travels life's road, one must remember there are hurdles and a myriad of challenges to overcome. Sometimes these trials come in great numbers. When this happens, one has to find strength in faith, hope, and prayers.

The first great milestone Carver reached was receiving a high school diploma, but he still yearned for more education. He learned about Highland University. He filed an application and submitted an essay to fulfill admission requirements. He was elated to receive a letter of acceptance.

Life is often filled with a combination of joy and pain. First came the joy as Carver read the acceptance letter and looked forward to his journey to college. The letter instructed him to report to Highland College on September 15.

But the fire of his jubilant spirits soon turned into a pile of ashes when he was turned away from Highland once the school president realized he was black. Dr. Otis, as he continued telling the story, said Carver would sometimes reflect on Proverbs 16:18 when he told the story of his disappointment: "Pride comes before the fall." In preparation for his new college life, he had dispensed with some of his belongings, keeping only what he needed. Now he had to start all over again.

When one is seeking to complete one's assignment in life, one has to remember to carry a basket of tenacity, persistence, hope, and prayers. Carver in this disappointing situation had to look beyond human ways and continue on with divine guidance. You can probably reflect on some unexpected pathways you have encountered in pursuit of goals, but what is most important is for one to remain focused on the goal. Think about George Washington Carver! The college president who turned him away had classified his essay as one of the best in the Minneapolis High School, but upon realizing the candidate was black, he struggled with issues related to class and tradition. There were no black students on the campus and, to his knowledge, none had applied for admission before.

Carver had been dealt a staggering blow. What was most painful to him was how he was being judged by physical qualities and not by his intelligence. As Dr. Otis told the story, "Carver wanted to leave that building as quickly as possible to find a quiet place where he could freely release his emotions, but as Carver placed his hands on the doorknob, the president revealed his inner thoughts. He was curious about why a black man in 1884, was not satisfied with achieving a high school education." The students listened carefully with appreciation as Dr. Otis described the scene. Carver knew God had identified a purpose for his life, and he believed God would guide him to completion. Carver responded to the president, "Time belongs to God. I am going to college because there is work for me to do and I must be ready."

What if Dr. Carver had given up the struggle of seeking to embrace his assignment to prepare himself to fulfill his mission? There would not have been a great science department at Armstrong Hall on the Tuskegee campus, and the world would be without the legacy of Dr. George Washington Carver. The lesson for each one of us is to identify one's purpose, embrace the assignment each is given, and stay the course to complete the mission.

Carver did not allow the college rejection to destroy his mission in life. He engaged in homesteading out west for a few years and finally met some people who directed him on his college pathway. In 1894, he became the first black to receive his bachelor's degree from Iowa State Agricultural and Mechanical College. In 1896, he received his master's degree and was invited to join the faculty. Dr. George Washington Carver stayed the course to develop his gifts to fulfill his mission to uplift humanity. He found his permanent home in 1896, fulfilling his mission at Tuskegee Institute until the close of his life in 1943.

George Washington Carver Time Line

1859   His brother, Jim, is born.

1864   Carver is born during the summer in Diamond Grove, Missouri. His father dies in a wagon accident before his birth.

1874   Grasshopper invasion[13]

1876   Leaves home to begin schooling in Neosho, Missouri.

1879   Witnesses the lynching of a black man in Fort Scott, Kansas, on March 26.

1883   Brother Jim dies of smallpox.

1884   Graduates from high school in Minneapolis, Kansas.

1886   Files claim on a homestead

1888   Quits homesteading after blizzard.

1889   Travels to Winterset, Iowa; works as a hotel cook; meets John and Helen Milholland, who inspire him to attend Simpson College in Indianola, Iowa.

1890   Enters Simpson College; meets Etta Budd, whose father admits him to his school.

1891   Transfers to Iowa Agricultural College and Model Farm.

1892   Art Show in Cedar Rapids, Iowa; publishes first scientific paper, "Grafting the Cacti."

1893   Exhibits his oil on linen, "Yucca and Cactus," inspired by his homesteading days, to represent the Hawkeye State at the World's Fair in Chicago.

1894   Receives bachelor's degree from Iowa Agricultural College; is admitted to graduate school on Nov. 14; receives prize for "Best Bulbs for the Amateur" from the Iowa Horticulture Society; writes senior thesis, "Plants Modified By Man," describing state-of-the-art work in grafting and cross-breeding plums, trees, geraniums, and amaryllis to improve fruit, vigor, and appearance.[14]

1895   Receives invitation from Booker T. Washington.

1896   Receives master of agriculture degree from Iowa Agricultural College, begins teaching at the Tuskegee Institute in Alabama.

1897   U.S. Secretary of Agriculture James Wilson visits Tuskegee; President William McKinley and cabinet visit Tuskegee.

1905   July 15 Farmer's Picnic theme: "Is it our duty to educate our children?"

1906   Farmers Conference at Tuskegee

1915   Bulletin: "When, What, and How to Can and Preserve Fruits and Vegetables in the Home," death of Booker T. Washington on Nov. 14.

1915   Boll Weevil threatens cotton crops.

1916   Elected Fellow of the Royal Society for the Encouragement of Arts in London.

1918   "How to Grow the Tomato and 115 Ways to Prepare it for the Table"

1920s   Experiments with legumes.

1921   Speaks before Congress on behalf of the protective tariff for peanut growers on Jan. 20.

1922   Receives the Spingarn Medal for Distinguished Service to Science from the National Association for the Advancement of Colored People.

1925   "How to Grow the Peanut and 105 Ways of Preparing it for Human Consumption"

1928   Receives Honorary Doctor of Science degree from Simpson College.

1920s—1930s   Corresponds with automobile maker Henry Ford, Thomas Alva Edison, and Mahatma Gandhi.

1929   Sculptress Isabel Schulz is commissioned to create a bronze wall plaque for Tuskegee.

1930s   Experiments with the soybean.

1936   "How the Farmer Can Save His Sweet Potatoes," addressing the industrial use of crops, known as chemurgy

1937   Bronze bust, June

1938   Receives Roosevelt Medal for outstanding contribution to southern agriculture.

1939   President Franklin D. Roosevelt receives a bottle of Carver's peanut massage oil during a visit on March 31. Carver receives the Roosevelt Medal, established in 1923 to honor people who have distinguished themselves in fields, associated with the career of President Theodore Roosevelt.

1941   George Washington Carver Museum opens at Tuskegee Institute.

1942   Henry Ford gives Carver a fully equipped laboratory for food research. Guests eat sandwiches and salads made by Carver from weeds and wild vegetables. 1943 Dies on January 5. Congress creates the George Washington Carver National Monument in Diamond Grove, Missouri.

CHAPTER 9

DOROTHEA DIX

A Social Reformer for the Mentally Ill and Prison Inmates

Place: Hampden, Maine; Worcester, Massachusetts; Canada, and Europe
Parents: Joseph Dix, a religious leader who distributed tracts, and Mary Bigelow Dix
Born: April 4, 1802
Died: July 17, 1887, in Trenton, New Jersey

Purpose
Dorothea was the eldest of three children born to Joseph and Mary Bigelow Dix in Hampden, Maine. The family lineage could be traced back to the Massachusetts Bay Colony. Dorothea's father was an itinerant Methodist teacher, and Dorothea often assisted him in distributing tracts throughout the community.[1] This work played an important role in sensitizing her to the needs of people in various walks of life. She also, however, experienced the pain of observing her parents become addicted to alcohol. Fortunately for her, she was the granddaughter of Dorothea Lynne, who was married to Dr. Elijah Dix and resided in Boston. At the age of twelve, Dorothea relocated there to live with her wealthy grandmother.[2]

In 1821, Dix transformed her grandmother's barn into a school for teaching poor and neglected children. To enrich her program, she began writing devotional books and stories for her students.

Assignment

One may venture into several types of work before identifying one's mission in life. Dix found herself involved in many brief assignments. In a sense, she and George Washington Carver were health challenged, but they overcame their obstacles.

Dix suffered from tuberculosis and traveled to Liverpool, England, to recover. She remained in England for eighteen months.[3] While there, she became interested in helping the mentally ill and envisioned the career path she wished to follow. As she attended meetings on mental-health care and engaged in conferences and social dialogue on the topic, she came to understand her purpose in life. Upon returning to America, she wasted no time in opening new doors to begin her work in the mental-health profession.

Mission

The breakthrough in identifying her mission came when she took a trip to Europe recommended by her physician. [4] There, she met those who felt government should play a direct, active role in social welfare. A movement for the reformation of care for the mentally ill was underway in Great Britain and included investigations into madhouses and asylums with reports made to the House of Commons.[5] Dix, in search of health restoration in Great Britain, found her life mission as a social reformer for the mentally ill.

She returned to America to research the needs of the mentally ill population there. In 1840 and 1841, she conducted a statewide investigation into the treatment of the impoverished mentally ill population in Massachusetts. After doing her research, she published the results in a report, known as a memorial, to the state legislature. "I proceed,

Gentlemen, briefly to call your attention to the present state of insane Persons (*sic*) confined within this Commonwealth, in cages, stalls, pens! Chained, naked, beaten with rods, and lashed into obedience."[6]

Dorothea Dix was successful in winning the attention of the legislature. Her report and lobbying motivated the legislators to enact a law to expand the state's mental hospital in Worcester.

Courage

Dix was deeply influenced by the work with the mentally ill population she observed in Great Britain. She returned to America with a new mission: she would implement this program in America. Dix spent a full year doing research. She was appalled at the horrendous conditions she discovered on personal visits to the asylums. She took courage to expose the situation and publish her findings, and she did not stop until her report was presented to the Worcester Legislature. When God transferred Moses's staff to Joshua, he told him three times to be strong and of good courage. The importance of courage was also emphasized to Jeremiah. "Be strong and of good courage" (Josh. 1:6). Dorothea Dix, too, needed courage to fulfill her mission.

Obstacles

Dix knew she could not initiate a change with words alone. She involved herself in active work to expose the problems she found. She wrote letters and took walking tours of the various cells and other locations where the indolent and insane population was housed. She designed a survey and presented a written report. Upon completing her research, she presented her case before the legislature. Dix's research was thorough and complete. She travelled across the nation to initiate services for the mentally ill population.

Divine Connection

Circumstances in her life prepared her for the work God wanted her to do. He readied her for her mission as she distributed tracts with her father, spent time with her grandmother, and discussed social reform during her visit in England. Upon embracing her divine assignment, Dorothea Dix began her research in order to expose the needs of the mentally ill to state legislatures. In 1844, she visited jails and almshouses in New Jersey and reported her findings to the legislature there.[7]

Her zeal for establishing proper facilities for the mentally ill took her from one end of America to the other. There was no state too small or too large for her to visit. This was the mission she embraced to the close of her life.

Gifts and Talents

Dix was an educator, a social reformer, and an activist for prison inmates and the mentally ill. She was deeply committed to the downtrodden in society.

Faith

She developed her faith during her childhood. She was often a surrogate mother for her younger siblings. Passing out tracts in the community gave her an opportunity to witness the faith of others. She had faith that God had a purpose for her life, and regardless of the struggles brought on by illness and family concerns, she knew she would come to realize her life's mission.

Summary

Born in Hampden, Maine, in 1802, Dorothea Lynde Dix was confronted with challenges, but she was persistent. She was so concerned about the suffering that she became a social reformer, devoting her talents and gifts to addressing the needs of the mentally ill and the inmates behind prison walls. After seeing the deplorable conditions in a Massachusetts prison, she spent the next forty years working toward the establishment of state hospitals for the mentally ill. Her efforts were instrumental in the creation of thirty-two institutions in the United States.[8]

CHAPTER 10

James V. Bennett

Rehabilitated American Prisons from the Years After World War I to 1964

I chose prison.
—James Bennett

Theme: Rehabilitate prisons. "Am I My Brother's Keeper?"
Founder of the Bureau of Prisons
American penal reformer
Place: USA
Born: August 29, 1894, in Silver Creek, New York
Died: November 19, 1978
Positions: Director of the Federal Bureau of Prisons in 1937-1964
Assistant Director of the Bureau from 1930-1937
US Army Air Corps veteran of World War I
Investigator for the US Bureau of Efficiency in 1919
Publication written in 1928

Purpose

Bennett received an honorable discharge from the army at the close of World War I in 1919. He married his sweetheart, and when he returned to America, his first obligation was to secure employment. He passed the civil service exam and was offered a position in the correctional system. Bennett also enrolled at George Washington University to pursue a law degree, which he received in 1926. He was assigned to the U.S. Bureau of Efficiency, a forerunner of the Hoover Commission and made an important connection when he met Herbert Brown, chief of the bureau. "Would you like to be assigned to the Department of Justice to study the federal prison system?" Brown asked. The chief explained the purpose of the study would be to show how the country could save money by putting idle federal prisoners to work. Bennett wanted to do more research on prisons before accepting this assignment. He talked to people and did extensive reading to gain knowledge about the prison system. Finally, he requested a prison tour. He chose the Ohio prison, one of the four largest prisons in the nation.

Assignment

The warden assigned a guide to give Bennett a tour of the Ohio prison. There were so many horrific sights, however, that Bennett cut the tour short.[1] In recounting the events to his wife, he blurted out, "I don't know why I have to be my brother's keeper!" She responded with a challenge: "Why not be your brother's keeper?" His conversation with his wife inspired him to take the assignment and to answer her question in a way that would set a new course for his life: "I chose prison."

Mission

The tour of the prison was a challenge for Bennett, but it turned his heart toward embracing his life mission. Brown invited him to join the Department of Justice staff to study the federal prison system.[2]

Courage

Bennett's tour through the Ohio prison stirred up strong feelings in him. Challenged by his wife, he took courage and began his assignment. He was inspired to write a plan for prison reform. In a brief time, he could write, "I chose prison." He found his assignment and embraced this as his mission in life. If he had surrendered to fear, Bennett would not have accomplished his great work in reforming American prisons. He became the founder of the federal Bureau of Prisons and accomplished a tremendous reduction in the prison population before he retired in 1964.

Divine Connection

When Brown offered him an assignment at the Department of Justice to study the federal prison system, a divine connection was made, putting Bennett in place to begin his mission and his life work—prison reform.

Faith

The prison tour in Ohio was a great challenge to Bennett. "Warden Thomas hurried me on down the corridor to the cells reserved for prisoners who refused to work or were otherwise recalcitrant," he said. "These men stood for hours or days in tiny strap-iron cages, in which there was no room to sit down, until they agreed to go back to work. I did not argue with the warden or ask any more questions. I had seen enough, and I never wanted to get out of a place so badly in my life."[3]

He viewed so many horrific scenes that he could not complete his tour. When his wife, Marie, asked him about the tour, he could only describe the painfully inhumane sights. Marie had done social work in Harlem and was excited about the concept of prison reform. She refused to let Bennett throw his hands up in despair.[4] She challenged him to walk by faith.

Summary

James V. Bennett served in the U.S. Army Air Corps during World War I. When World War I ended, Bennett found employment with the U.S. Bureau of Efficiency in 1919.

Bennett was introduced to Sanford Bates, the famous international prison reformer. Bates had years of experience working with inmates in other countries. He promoted a plan to rehabilitate inmates with educational reform. He believed punishment was out of date and criminality could be treated as if it were an illness.[5] Bennett was given the opportunity to work with Bates as assistant director of the bureau from 1930 to 1937. As he observed Bates, Bennett began formulating his own ideas and envisioning programs he wanted to see implemented to achieve prison reform.

Bennett wanted to make prison time count. The prisons, in his opinion, should be rehabilitative. He wanted inmates to be taught life skills to help them survive upon re-entering society. He also felt a deep need to address the needs of mentally and physically ill inmates. In 1928, Bennett published "The Federal Penal and Correctional Problem," calling for a new centralized prison bureau and leading to the creation of the federal Bureau of Prisons (BOP). After years of observing the living conditions and day-to-day routine of prisoners, Bennett was convinced of the need for prison reform. In his opinion, the prisons had become inhumane and were operated poorly.

Franklin D. Roosevelt entered the White House in 1933, ratified the Hoover charters for prison reform, and reappointed Bates and three assistant directors, including Bennett, to the Bureau of Prisons. In 1937, Bates resigned, and Bennett was appointed director by Roosevelt.

Bennett began implementing his program for change. Recommendations were made for the construction of two more prisons and a home for the mentally ill as well as for the implementation of services for those addicted to alcohol and drugs. Bennett called for the establishment of a full-time federal board of parole.

When Bennett retired in 1964, the American prison system was greatly improved. Statistics from The Correctional Association of New York in February 1995 tells a story of change: **"In January 1973 there were 12,500 persons in the State prison system. Today there are over 58,000."**

FACT SHEET: TRENDS IN U.S. CORRECTIONS

Trends in U.S. Corrections

U.S. State and Federal Prison Population, 1925-2016

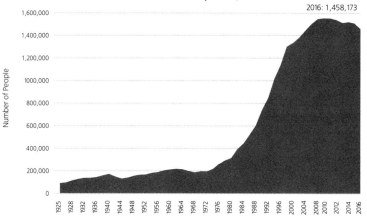

2016: 1,458,173

Source: Bureau of Justice Statistics *Prisoners Series.*

International Rates of Incarceration per 100,000

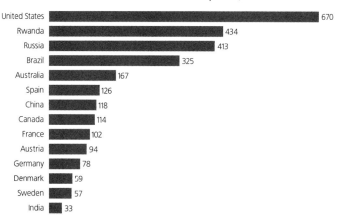

Country	Rate
United States	670
Rwanda	434
Russia	413
Brazil	325
Australia	167
Spain	126
China	118
Canada	114
France	102
Austria	94
Germany	78
Denmark	59
Sweden	57
India	33

Source: Walmsley, R. (2018). World Prison Brief. London: Institute for Criminal Policy Research. Available online: http://www.prisonstudies.org/world-prison-brief

The Sentencing Project • 1705 DeSales Street NW, 8th Floor • Washington, D.C. 20036 • sentencingproject.org

What if James V. Bennett were permitted to revisit the prisons in America? He would be surprised to see the growth of prisons in the nation. China has twenty percent of the world's population and the USA has only five percent. The Walmsley World Prison Brief (10ᵗʰ edition) lists **America with an average daily prison population of 2,239,751, the highest in the Western world**. Jed S. Rakoff in "Mass Incarceration: The Silence of the Judges" *echoes a population of* "more than 2.2 million people who are currently incarcerated in US jails and prisons, a 500 percent increase over the past forty years."[6] Bennett would probably smile as he studies carefully the trends in US corrections as presented in The Sentencing Project[7] map showing prison growth from 1925 to 2016. I am sure he would make a few critical observations. He would easily note the percentage growth of prisons from 1925 to 1976. Then Bennett would probably become appalled at the skewed, aggressive rise in prisons from the 1980s to 2012. As he proceeds with his study of the prison system, he would want to write another manual for reform. I am certain his eyes would widen in disbelief when he views The Sentencing Project Map for 1925-2016. He would immediately seek to identify the isolated factor that is contributing to the aggressive growth as a cancer, swelling the prison population in twenty-first century America.

In his contemporary research, Bennett would identify the direct correlation between private prisons emerging as prisons for profit in the 1980s and the skewing of prison population figures from their natural cycles of growth. In studying the most current statistics, Bennett would probably note the drastic *decrease in the violent prison population* after the 1990s and the sporadic increase in the nonviolent inmate population. His serious question would be, "What is that aggregate factor that is out of control?" He would also recognize some trends that contribute to prison growth. He would want to look at the composition of inmates locked behind the prison walls to research the question "why?" These investigations would guide him in understanding the aggregate factor contributing to prison growth. What is that factor that has been causing the increase in the prison population since the 1980s? He would want to view some data and pull some records to understand what has caused this drastic populational shift from a normal prison growth rate in 1925 to the 1970s where an alarming, out-of-control prison population has been increasing from the late 1980s to 2018.

In his research, Bennett would note the two largest private prisons for profit were incorporated in 1983, showing a direct correlation to aggressive prison growth in the nation. He would further note some other critical findings. February 1998 stats from The Correctional Association of New York reveal the following:

Prisoner Profile in New York
- Addicted Population: "60-70% of inmates—38,400 to 44,800—have a history of drug abuse."
- Illiterate Population: "75% of prisoners have no high school diploma."
- Drugs: "About 60% of the offenders sent to State prison in 1993 were convicted of *non-violent crimes.*"

The Correctional Association of New York, March 2004 statistics reveal: "In recent years the State has used more and more prison space for drug and other non-violent offenders and less for violent offenders. In 1980, 886 drug offenders were sent to State prison, 11% of the total court commitments for that year. By 2003 the number of drug offenders sent to State prison had reached 6,540, 37.7% of the total. In contrast: the number of violent offenders sent to State prison in 1983 was 7,926, 63% of total court commitments; in 2003 the number of violent offenders going upstate was 5,116, 29.5% of the total."
- City Jails: "Only 10 % of the City inmates have a high school or equivalency diploma."
- The Correctional Association of New York February 1995 stats reveal:

- "As of December 31, 1994, there were 8,433 drug offenders locked up in NYS prisons under the Rockefeller Drug Laws. It costs nearly $253 million per year to keep these offenders imprisoned."
- Racial Composition: "Studies and experience have shown that the majority of people who use and sell drugs in NYS and the nation are white."
- "African-Americans and Latinos comprise 93.8% of the drug offenders in NYS prisons. African Americans, 47.4%; Latinos, 46.4%; *whereas whites make up only 5.7%.*"
- As of November 1994: "Between 1986 and 1991, the number of women in state prisons grew 75%. The increase in sentenced *drug offenders* accounted for 55% of this growth."

Bennett would turn his attention to some periodicals to further understand why the map is skewed from the 1980s to 2012. A quick look into the "why question" would lead him to thumb through a few pages in the periodicals to identify some causal factors for this artificial growth in the prison population. In searching for causes, he might peruse articles by Eric Schlosser and Vicky Pelaez to get a description of contributing factors in twenty-first-century USA.

In "The Prison-Industrial Complex" in *The Atlantic*, December 1998, Schlosser gives a description of twenty-first-century prisons. "The prison-industrial complex is not only a set of interest groups and institutions. It is a state of mind," Schlosser writes. "The lure of money is corrupting the nation's criminal-justice system, replacing notions of public service with a drive for higher profits."[8] Bennett would note his work in reforming the prisons before his retirement in 1964. He was a defender of public service. He wanted to rehabilitate and train inmates to prepare them for re-entry to society, helping them to become productive citizens by using their gifts and talents to contribute to society in a positive manner.

Schlosser's article reveals a negative change of heart. Schlosser writes that the "eagerness of elected officials to pass 'tough on crime' legislation—combined with their unwillingness to disclose the true costs of these laws—has encouraged all sorts of financial improprieties." Bennet's work was so thorough until Congress in the 1970s considered closing some federal prisons (in Georgia, Kansas, and Washington). I am sure Bennett would place great importance on the question of what has caused this swift change in prison growth in the 1980s. Schlosser writes that the prison growth began in New York and moved into other regions of the nation. **Dorothy R. Swygert in *Silence in a Democracy: Prisons for Profit: 21st Century Modern-day Slavery* shows how prison growth** expanded in the administrations of four New York governors—Nelson Rockefeller, Hugh Carey, Mario Cuomo, and George Pataki.[9]

Nelson A. Rockefeller opened the prison pathway with the introduction of his Rockefeller Drug Laws in New York in January 1973.

Hugh Carey prepared the financial pathway to embrace prisons when he convinced the Legislature in 1975 to convert the Urban Development Corporation, originally designed to address a housing shortage for low-income neighborhoods, into a body with a new mission to finance other state projects. **It was then sometimes used by governors to circumvent formal legislative or voter scrutiny.**

Mario Cuomo's work set a new model for the prison industry. A Correctional Association of New York report from February 1995 reveals that "Starting in 1983, the Cuomo Administration built over 33,000 prison spaces, more than the number built by all previous administrations combined." When he completed his three terms of office, Cuomo had spent more than seven billion on the prison building program. Ann Richardson, governor of Texas, used his model and it went viral, spreading to California and states across the nation.

George Pataki embraced the prison expansion plan in New York. In "New York State of Mind?: Higher Education vs. Prison Funding in the Empire, 1988-1998," the authors, Robert Gangi, Vincent Schiraldi and Jason Ziedenberg presents a broad perspective of Pataki's priorities.

> **"On April 26, [1998] Gov.** Pataki vetoed $500 million for school construction, $77 million for teacher salary enhancement, and cut $17.32 million from the State University of New York's (SUNY) budget, and $8.6 million from the City University of New York's (CUNY) BUDGET, AND $ 8.6 million from SUNY, and $7.5 million from CUNY for the hiring of more faculty, and $13.5 million for a program that would have given students a $65 credit for textbook purchases. **These figures show that, rather than pursuing new priorities and new ideas of governance, Gov. Pataki has continued 'business as usual' in feeding the growing behemoth of prison cell, at the expense of classrooms."**[10]

We salute Robert Gangi, Vincent Schiraldi, and Jason Zeidenberg for their ongoing research to make the public aware of this fatal trend of prison expansion at the expense of fulfilling educational needs. This type system is a replication of the slavery institution in America which prohibited slaves from being educated. The most serious offense is the denial of humanity to develop their gifts and talents to live productive lives.

Schlosser says "the inner workings of the prison-industrial complex can be observed in the state of New York, where the prison boom started, transforming the economy of an entire region; in Texas and Tennessee, where private prison companies have thrived; and in California, where the correctional trends of the past two decades have converged and reached extremes."

Bennett would have, strategically gathered, information about the aggregate factor causing a continuous artificial growth in the prison population. I imagine he would want to understand the cause. In studying the periodicals more fully, he would want to view the work of another writer, Vicky Pelaez, whose article is entitled, "The Prison Industry in the United States: Big Business or a New Form of Slavery?"[11] Pelaez wastes no time in identifying twenty-first-century prison growth in America. Eyes from around the globe of human rights organizations are on the USA, condemning her for inhumane exploitation. Palaez resounds the global viewpoint, defining USA prisons as inhumane exploitation, "where they say a prison population of up to 2 million – mostly black and Hispanic – are working for various industries for a pittance." Who are the benefactors of this cheap labor and what is the great value? "For the tycoons who have invested in the prison industry," as the song from human rights organizations continues through the voice of Pelaez, "it has been like finding a pot of gold. They don't have to worry about strikes or paying unemployment insurance, vacations or comp time. All of their workers are full-time and never arrive late or are absent because of family problems; moreover, if they don't like the pay of 25 cents an hour and refuse to work, they are locked up in isolation cells."

James V. Bennett would look at his watch and see it was time to go. He would place his hand upon his heart and say, "A monumental task for this generation! For me, I Chose Prisons as my purpose, my mission, and my assignment. Now I pass the cloak to the current generation to make a difference on God's earth."[12]

BIBLIOGRAPHY

Adams, Russell. *Great Negroes Past and Present.* Chicago: Afro American
    Publishing, 1963.

Adler, David A. *A Picture Book of George Washington Carver.* New York:
    Holiday House, 1999.

Albus, Harry James. *The Peanut Man: The Life of George Washington
    Carver in Story Form.*

Grand Rapids, MI: W. B. Eerdmans Publishing Co., 1948.

American National Biography. Vol. 4. New York: Oxford University
    Press, 1999.

Bennett, Scott H. *Radical Pacifism: The War Resisters League and Gandhian
    Nonviolence in America, 1915-1963.* Syracuse: Syracuse University
    Press, 2003.

Bolden, Tonya. *George Washington Carver.* New York: Abrams Books
    for Young Readers in New York, 2008.

Bradford, Sarah H. *Scenes in the Life of Harriet Tubman* Auburn,
    NY: W.J. Moses, 1869. https://archive.org/stream/
    scenesinlifeofha00bradrich?ref=ol#page/no

Briska, William. *The History of Elgin Mental Health Center: Evolution
    of a State Hospital.*

    Carpentersville, IL: Crossroads Communications, 1997.

Buchard, Peter Duncan. *Carver: Great Soul.* Fairfax, CA: Wise as Serpents
    Harmless as Doves, 1998.

Buchard, Peter Duncan, principal investigator. *George Washington Carver: For His Times and Ours. Special History Study: Natural History Related to George Washington Carver National Monument.* National Park Service, United States Department of the Interior, 2005.

Clinton, Catharine. *Reminiscences of My Life in Camp: An African American Woman's Civil War.* Athens, GA: University of Georgia Press, 2006.

Coil, Suzanne M. *George Washington Carver.* New York: F. Watts, 1990.

Conrad, Earl. *Harriet Tubman: Negro Soldier and Spy.* New York: International Publishers Co., 1942.

Doeden, Matt. *George Washington Carver.* New York: Lerner Publications Company, 2007.

Du Bois, W.E.B. *Black Reconstruction in America, 1860-1880.* New York: Simon & Schuster, 1998.

Donald, David Herbert. *Charles Sumner and the Rights of Man.* New York: Open Road Media, 2016.

Driscoll, Laura. *George Washington Carver: The Peanut Wizard.* New York: Grosset & Dunlop, 2003.

Edwards, Ethel. *Carver of Tuskegee.* The National Park Service, 1976.

Elliott, Lawrence. *George Washington Carver: The Man Who Overcame.* Englewood Cliffs, NJ: Prentice Hall, 1966.

Goldenberg, Barry M. *The Unknown Architects of Civil Rights: Thaddeus Stevens, Ulysses S. Grant.* Los Angeles: Critical Minds Press, 2011. EPUB, Mobile for Kindle.

Harlan, Louis R., ed. *The Booker T. Washington Papers.* Champaign, IL: University of Illinois Press.

Hill, Roy L. *Booker T's Child.* Washington, DC, 1993.

"Historic Missourians: George Washington Carver" in *Dictionary of American Biography,* Supplement 3, New York: Charles Scribner's Sons, 1973.

Hoch, Bradley R. *Thaddeus Stevens in Gettysburg: The Making of an Abolitionist.* Ritzville, WA: Adams County Historical Society, 2005.

Holt, Rackham. *George Washington Carver: An American Biography.* Garden City, NY:

Doubleday, Doran and Company, 1943.

Hughes, Langston. *A Pictorial History of the Negro.* New York: Crown Publishers, 1956.

Kremer, Gary R. *George Washington Carver: A Biography.* Santa Barbara, CA: Greenwood, 2011.

Kremer, Gary R., ed. *George Washington Carver in His Own Words.* Columbia, MO: University of Missouri Press, 1987.

Lawson, Elizabeth. *Thaddeus Stevens: Militant Democrat and Fighter for Negro Rights.* Portland, ME: Blackstone Audio, 2013.

Lewis, David Levering. *W.E.B Du Bois: The Fight for Equality and the American Century, 1919-1963.* New York: Henry Holt and Company, 2001.

McMurry, Linda O. *George Washington Carver, Scientist and Symbol.* New York: Oxford University Press, 1981.

Merritt, Raleigh H. *From Captivity to Fame: Or the Life of George Washington Carver.*

Boston: Meador Publishing Company, 1929.

Michel, Sonya. "Dorothea Dix; or, the Voice of the Maniac." *Discourse: Journal for Theoretical Studies in Media and Culture* 17, no. 2, Digital Commons.

Norrell, Robert. *Up From Slavery: The Life of Booker T. Washington.* Cambridge: Belknap Press, 2009.

Puleo, Stephen. *The Caning: The Assault That Drove America to Civil War.* Yardley, PA: Westholme Publishing, 2013.

Swygert, Dorothy R. *Healing the Nation: An In-depth Study of African Americans.* Hampton, VA: Rekindle the Heart Publishers, 2005.

Swygert, Dorothy R. *Silence in a Democracy: Prisons for Profit*: 21st Century Modern-day Slavery Hampton, VA: Rekindle the Heart Publishers, 2016.

Thomas, Henry. *George Washington Carver.* New York: G. P. Putnam's Sons, 1958.

Tiffany, Francis. *Life of Dorothea Lynde Dix.* Boston: Houghton Mifflin Company, 1890.

Washington, Booker T. *Character Building.* New York: Doubleday, Page & Co., 1902.

Washington, Booker T. *The Negro in Business.* Wichita, KS: Devore & Sons, 1992.

Washington, Booker T. *Up From Slavery.*

Wellman, Sam. *George Washington Carver.* Newton, KS: Wild Centuries Press, 1998.

Yarbrough, William Henry. *A History of the United States for High Schools.* New York: Laidlaw Brothers Publishers, 1941.

Notes

CHAPTER 3: ABIGAIL ADAMS

1   "Abigail Adams," Dictionary of Unitarian and Universalist Biography, Unitarian Universalist History and Heritage Society, posted February 28, 2001, http://uudb.org/articles/abigailadams.html. Retrieved through web.archive.org.

2   Mable Casner, *Story of the American Nation,* (New York: Harcourt, Brace & World, Inc., 1962), 232.

3   Swygert, *Silence in a Democracy: Prisons for Profit*: 21st Century Modern-day Slavery, 44.

4   John Hope Franklin, *From Slavery to Freedom* (New York: Alfred Knopf, 1967), 129.

5   John Adams Heritage, John Adams Historical Society, http://www.john-adams-heritage.com.
Rice on History, Daniel Rice, https://riceonhistory.wordpress.com.
Wikipedia, Wikimedia Foundation, https://www.wikipedia.org.
Encyclopedia Brittanica, Brittanica, https://www.britannica.com.

6   John Adams to Abigail Adams, 26 April 1777, Adams Family Papers, Massachusetts Historical Society, quoted in *Adams Family Correspondence,* Vol. 12. (Cambridge, Massachusetts: Belknap Press of Harvard University Press, 1963.)

CHAPTER 4: HARRIET TUBMAN

1   Bradford, *Scenes in the Life of Harriet Tubman*, 19.

2   "Harriet Tubman," Wikipedia, Wikimedia Foundation, https://en.wikipedia.org/wiki/Harriet_Tubman.

3   Ibid.

4   Ibid.

5   Ibid.

CHAPTER 5: THADDEUS STEVENS

1   "Thaddeus Stevens," Wikipedia, Wikimedia Foundation, https://en.wikipedia.org/wiki/Thaddeus_Stevens.

2   ibid.

3   ibid.

4   Swygert, *Silence in a Democracy: Prisons for Profit*: 21st Century Modern-day Slavery, 10.

5   "Thaddeus Steven," Wikipedia.

6   Ibid.

7   Ibid.

8   "Forty Acres and a Mule—The Elusive Promise," American History USA, March 6, 2012. https://www.americanhistoryusa.com/forty-acres-and-a-mule-elusive-promise/.

9   Swygert, *Silence in a Democracy: Prisons for Profit: 21st Century Modern-day Slavery,* 68.

10   "Thaddeus Stevens," Military Wiki, FANDOM.

11   "Thaddeus Stevens," Manly Wiki, FANDOM, http://manly.wikia.com/wiki/Thaddeus_Stevens.

CHAPTER 6: CHARLES SUMNER

1   "Charles Sumner," Wikipedia, Wikimedia Foundation, https://en.wikipedia.org/wiki/Charles_Sumner.

2   Ibid.

3   Ibid.

4   Ibid.

5   Kenneth N. Addison, *We Hold These Truths to be self-Evident . . .* (Lan-

ham, MD: University Press of America, Inc., 2009), xxii.

6   Swygert, *Silence in a Democracy: Prisons for Profit*: 21ˢᵗ Century Modern-day Slavery.

7   Ibid, 80.

8   "Charles Sumner," Wikipedia.

9   Ibid.

10   Ibid.

11   Yarbrough, *A history of the United States for High Schools*, 212.

"He has waged cruel war against human nature itself, violating its most sacred rights of life and liberty in the persons of a distant people who never offended him, captivating and carrying them into slavery in another hemisphere, or to incur miserable death in their transportation. This piratical warfare is the warfare of the Christians King of Great Britain. Determine to keep open a market where men should be bought and sold, he has prostituted his negative for suppressing every legislative attempt to prohibit or to restrain … commerce."

This clause was in the original writing of The Declaration of Independence. The same document was deleted because Southern colonies demanded the retraction. If this corollary had remained in the Declaration of Independence, the slaves would have received their freedom with the colonists in 1783.

12   Everipedia, Everipedia., Inc., https://everipedia.org, accessed February 2, 2018.

13   "Charles Sumner," Wikipedia.

14   Ibid. POLITICO website, https://www.politico.com/.

15   Charles Sumner," Wikipedia. Swygert, *Silence in a Democracy: Prisons for Profit: 21ˢᵗ Century Modern-day Slavery*, 81.

CHAPTER 7: BOOKER T. WASHINGTON

1   "Booker T. Washington," Wikipedia, Wikimedia Foundation, https://en.wikipedia.org/wiki/Booker_T._Washington.

"Wayland Seminary was the Washington, D.C. School of the National Theological Institute. The Institute was established beginning in 1865 by the American Baptist Home Mission Society (ABHMS). At first designed primarily for providing education and training for African American freedmen to enter into the ministry, it expanded its offerings to meet the educational demands of the former slave population. Just before the end of the 19th century, it was merged with its sister institution the Richmond Theological Seminary to form the current Virginia Union University at Richmond."

2   Ibid.

3   "National Negro Business League," Revolvy, https://www.revolvy.com/page/National-Negro-Business-League.

4   Russell Adams, *Great Negroes Past and Present*, 111.

5   Ibid.

6   Ibid.

7   Paulette Davis-Horton, *Death in 60 Days* (Bloomington, IN: Author-House, 2008), 83.

CHAPTER 8: GEORGE WASHIGTON CARVER

1   "George Washington Carver," Wikipedia, Wikimedia Foundation, https://en.wikipedia.org/wiki/George_Washington_Carver.

2   Ibid.

3   Ibid.

4   Ibid.

5   Ibid.

6   Ibid.

7   Ibid.

8   Ibid.

9   Ibid.

10   Ibid.

11   Ibid.
The Columbia Electronic Encyclopedia, Columbia University Press, www.cc.columbia.edu/cu/cup/.

12   Suzanne, M. Coil, *George Washington Carver* (New York: Franklin Watts Library Edition, 1990).

13   Wellman, *George Washington Carver*, 97.

14   Ibid, 193-4.

CHAPTER 9: DOROTHEA DIX

1   "Dorothea Dix," Wikipedia, Wikimedia Foundation, https://en.wikipedia.org/wiki/Dorothea_Dix.

2   Ibid.

3   Ibid.

4   Ibid.

5   Ibid.

6   Ibid.

7   Sonya Michel, "Dorothea Dix; or, The Voice of the Maniac," 48-66.

8   Ibid.

CHAPTER 10: JAMES V. BENNETT

1   Swygert, *Silence in a Democracy: Prisons for Profit*: 21st Century Modern–day Slavery, 229.

2   Ibid., 230.

3   Ibid., 231.

4   Ibid., 235.

5   Ibid.

6   Jed S. Rakoff, "Mass Incarceration: The Silence of the Judges," The New York Review of Books 67, no. 9, May 2015, 14-17.

7   The Sentencing Project, *Trends in U.S. Corrections,* (Washington D.C.).

8   Eric Schlosser, "The Prison-Industrial Complex," *The Atlantic,* December 1998, 1-9.

9   Swygert, *Silence in a Democracy: Prisons for Profit: 21st Century Modern-day Slavery.*

10   William Martin and Andy Pragacz, "Education and Incarceration in NYS, Recalculating the Fate of New York's Youth, from Cuomo to

Cuomo," Binghamton Justice Projects, June 2013.

11   Vicky Pelaez, *The Prison Industry in the United States: Big Business or a New Form of Slavery?"* Global Research, March 31, 2014.

12   James V. Bennett, "I Chose Prison," in *Reader's Digest Condensed Books* (Pleasantville, NY: Reader's Digest Association, 1970).

APPENDIX

STAGES IN IDENTIFYING YOUR PURPOSE IN LIFE

Birth Status
- Acknowledge your status at birth. (This may be symbolic of your mission.)
    - o What is unique about your early circumstances?
    - o Moses's birth circumstances were important to his story, as were those of George Washington Carver.

The Yearning
- Recognize the yearning stage as you identify your purpose.
    - o Unshakable Drive
    - o Nudging (Nagging)
    - o Unquenchable Desire
    - o Yearning

Recognition
- This is what you enjoy.
- This is what you are good at doing.
- These are your gifts and talents.

- This is how you can impact people in your career and other areas of your life.

Purpose/Identification
- Identification
- Recognition
- Acceptance
  - Your talents line up with your purpose in life.
  - Identify and fulfill your inner desire.

Preparation (Education, Apprenticeship, or Training)
- School, college, apprenticeships

The Challenge
- Endurance
  - Struggles
  - Challenges
  - Persistence
  - Fortitude
  - Faith

The Mission
- Your purpose compliments the talents and gifts you were given at birth. (See Matthew 25.)
- Your mission is your life's work in God's vineyard as you uplift humanity with your talents.

The Architect's Blueprint

God moves upon the heart and soul to reveal His will to an individual. As one listens to the quiet, still voice of the Creator, the process has begun of molding and shaping the individual for his/her journey in life.

An architect would define this as a blueprint. God is the architect who creates the blueprint for a person's life. The individual is to God as clay is to the potter. Shaping reveals the will of God in many aspects. In this spirit-driven process, the person's mind is like a sponge, absorbing the divine instructions of God. If the individual is obedient and flexible in obeying God's will, the process unfolds from one stage to the next. If there is resistance, the Potter may have to extend the period of teaching in order to further mold the individual to achieve his or her life's purpose.

Why does God
pave the pathway at birth?

The Calling

God paves the pathway of an individual at birth to maximize the impact of the gift and give the individual more time to work to achieve the mission. In Jeremiah 1:5, God describes the calling of Jeremiah. "Before I formed thee in the belly I knew thee; and before thou came forth out of the womb I sanctified thee, and I ordained thee a prophet unto the nations." Jeremiah's calling was to prophesy to all the nations; therefore, time was of the essence. His mission was of the highest importance, as specified in Jeremiah 1:7, which says, "… for thou shalt go to all that I shall send thee, and whatsoever I command thee thou shalt speak." Instructions and assurances were spoken as the mission was assigned. "Be not afraid of their faces: for I am with thee to deliver thee, saith the Lord" (Jer. 1:8).

Purpose and Mission

Jeremiah's calling to go and speak before the nations was his *purpose*. The *mission* was to make God's Word known to all nations, importuning them to live according to the law of God. Jeremiah was required to speak the message of God. "And I will utter my judgments against them touching all their wickedness, who have forsaken me, and have burned incense unto other gods, and worshipped the works of their own hands" (Jer. 1:16).

Courage

The individual must have courage, as God reveals in Jeremiah 1:19. "And they shall fight against thee; but they shall not prevail against thee; for I am with thee, saith the Lord, to deliver thee." Courage is a key quality. When God began the process of transferring power to Joshua, he admonished him three times about the need for courage in Joshua 1:6 as well as in chapters seven and nine. A similar message was given in Joshua 1:9: "Have not I commanded thee? Be strong and of a good courage; be not afraid, neither be thou dismayed: for the Lord thy God is with thee whithersoever thou goest."

The prophet Jeremiah was charged with delivering a message from the omnipotent God to man—a created creature. Therefore, this messenger from God had to possess indomitable courage. The prophet is charged by the almighty God and must not yield to any materialism of the day. Nothing was more important than delivering the message of "Thus saith the Lord." As seen in Moses's numerous visits to Pharaoh, he was under divine authority to deliver the message to the Egyptian leader.

Status at birth may also be an indicator of a person's mission. How did the birth status influence the lives of Moses, Booker T. Washington, and George Washington Carver?

Moses was born in Egypt to Israelite slaves Yochebed and Amram. Orders had been given for the killing of boys who were two and younger. Placed upon the Nile, the baby in the bulrush basket was found by the pharaoh's daughter, who embraced him as a gift from the Nile. Raised with the privileges of Egyptian court life, the infant was destined to lead the Israelites from their bondage to the pharaoh. Moses questioned the circumstances of his birth and was called into God's service.

Booker T. Washington was born into American slavery in 1856, was freed in 1865, and emerged as a leader to establish a school to help African Americans acquire the education and skills they needed to survive after the Civil War.

George Washington Carver was born in 1864, one year before the close of the Civil War. His mother, Mary, a slave girl in Moses Carver's household, was kidnapped along with her children. Moses Carver hired a neighbor to search for them, and baby George was discovered under a tree. Moses and his wife Susan met the challenge of restoring baby George back to health, but there were physical consequences of that kidnapping. Carver's voice remained high and shrill, and he suffered from respiratory issues for many years. Because of his physical challenges, his adopted mother kept him from strenuous farm work. Instead, he was trained to manage the household and was permitted to spend his leisure time in nature. The young boy taught himself to care for plants and flowers and learned how to restore them to health.

The Mission

Purpose complements talents, which are given at birth, as explained in Matthew, Chapter twenty-five. A person's mission is his or her life's work in God's vineyard as they uplift humanity with those gifts.

Find Your Purpose in Life

Theme:

Time:

Purpose:

Mission:

Courage:

Fortitude:

Divine Connection:

Assignment:

Persistence:

Faith:

Gifts and Talents:

PART II:
Helping Youth to Understand Their Purpose in Life

Why are you important? No one's birth is an accident.

You have received an assignment from the Creator to fulfill the mission for which you were placed upon this earth. Who will assist you in identifying your purpose in life? Where, along your journey, will you find signs to help you recognize your assignment? What is the time frame of your mission? How will you respond to challenges, which have an interesting way of pushing you toward your assignment? If we could guide youth through each stage of life to ensure their maximum growth and development, each child could hit their mark right away, realizing the purpose the Creator has for them.

On the Children

Kahlil Gibran

Your children are not your children,
They are the sons and daughters of Life's longing for itself.
They come through you but not from you,
And though they are with you, yet they belong not to you.

You may give them your love but not your thoughts,
For they have their own thoughts.
You may house their bodies but not their souls,
For their souls dwell in the house of tomorrow,
    which you cannot visit, not even in your dreams.

You may strive to be like them, but seek not to make them like you.
For life goes not backward nor tarries with yesterday.

You are the bows from which your children as living arrows are sent forth.
The archer sees the mark upon the path of the Infinite,
    and He bends you with His might that His arrows may go
    swift and far.
Let your bending in the archer's hand be for gladness.
For even as He loves the arrow that flies,
    So He loves also the bow that is stable.

BEGINNING THE JOURNEY

Youthful, bright, ebullient, and ready to begin your life—or so you think! You go from your parents' arms to the cradle, and soon you crawl and begin to walk. You are eager to explore life in this big gigantic world. There are so many things to learn and so many adaptations to make, but finally, you are on your way, crawling into the stage of pulling up on objects until you are ready to walk upright. We know there are variations from person to person as one begins experimenting in this enormous world. We will just address a few general challenges to get young people to start analyzing their purpose for being born into this world.

The Lebanese poet Kahlil Gibran paints a picture of how a person begins to live life on planet earth. In the poem, above, he emphasizes the immense role of the parent in teaching, training, and nurturing children. "You are the bows from which your children as living arrows are sent forth."

What is the role of the parent in molding and shaping the child from infancy to adulthood while preparing them to take their journey in life? Many books have been written and many lectures have been presented to shed light upon this discipline! Gibran likens parents and children to bows and arrows. The parents are as bows. The arrows are as infants sent into the world through the passageway of their parents. Who is the sender of these "arrows"? Gibran infers the arrows are sent forth through the bows by the Infinite. The Giver of Life, our Creator, is the Infinite. In this life-giving plan, each one has a role in the beginning, developing, and moral shaping of the human package, according to Gibran. "The archer sees the path of the Infinite, and He bends you with his might that His arrows may go swift and far." With the help of everyone from medical doctors to parents, teachers, and guidance counselors, the young person gradually becomes absorbed into the new environment.

Let us pause to carefully examine the role of the bows (parents). The archer (Creator) knows the origin of the birth as well as the purpose for which the arrow (child) is sent to planet earth by the Infinite, therefore, the arrow is sent for a specific purpose with a mission to fulfill between birth and death—an assignment from the Infinite. How can parents (bows) fulfill their role to insure the children (arrows) will go "swift and far" to reach the target of the Infinite (Creator)? What does Gibran infer with his words, "He bends you with his might that His arrows may go swift and far"? Let us take a quick glimpse into the psychological and sociological environment of child-rearing practices in our world. If parents and family life are stable, the arrow will go straight to the mark to reach the target and fulfill the mission set by the Infinite. As the poet says, "He bends you with his might that His arrows may go swift and far." In a challenging home environment, the arrow may ricochet, but in time it may return to the path designed at birth. It will, however, be left with less time to fulfill the mission. The worst scenario is that the arrow will reach the close of life without one ever realizing the purpose of one's birth. Where is the blame? Does it lie with the individual? Is the parent to blame? Is it the fault of society, or is it a combination of all three? Who is the lesser for the failure of an individual to fulfill the purpose he or she was assigned from birth? What is the role of society in helping to make this fulfillment a reality? What is the role of the parents? What is the role of the individual? Who is deprived of receiving a gift that is sent forth but unable to hit his or her mark upon the path of the Infinite?

In gift giving, the Infinite smiles upon the bows (parents) that are stable. For in this glad scenario, the arrows (children) may reach the full mark because parents and society have fulfilled their roles in uplifting humanity by nurturing children to be all the Creator would have them to be.

Yes, each person is born on this earth for a purpose. Each person has been given gifts and talents at birth to assist in their success. One may develop these gifts and talents by acquiring education in specific disciplines in preparation for fulfilling one's mission. I have the gift of nurturing children. In preparation for my assignment in this area, I had to earn degrees in education, but I had been endowed with my nurturing skills and love for children at birth.

What about you? Have you made an assessment to help you identify your gifts and talents? Do you want to understand why you were placed on this earth? What would you like to do or what would you like to contribute to humanity to help make this a better world? Sometimes I would do an oral survey with my students to challenge them to identify their talents. I often smiled at their responses. Some students would quickly tell me in a subtle voice, "I ain't got no talent!" I saw these responses as a challenge, and I would follow up with a few questions! "What do you mean you do not have a talent"? I would ask. "What are your hobbies? What do you do in your leisure time"?

This dialogue oftentimes motivated them to take a new look at themselves. They began to recognize skills and talents they had taken for granted. In recognition of this need, I have created some easy charts to help you make an appraisal of your gifts and talents. As you begin this assessment, you will start to identify some of the special skills that make you unique. Find a quiet time and a pleasant place where you can sit alone with your thoughts to identify your talents and the ways you would like to use them. Contemplate the ways you can make a difference in building a better world. Remember you were given these gifts at birth, and now you must work to develop your gifts to fulfill your purpose in life. Your gifts and talents were given to you to fulfill your purpose in life between birth and death. Certainly, you want to leave your best work behind for the next generation. Go for it! You are a great person with a great mission to fulfill.

Let us begin with the PURPOSE.

How to Identify **MY PURPOSE** in Life

To come to know your purpose is to find the reason for your existence. Your answers will resonate within your soul.

1. What are my gifts and talents?

   _____

   _____

   _____

2. How do I use my gifts and talents?

   _____

   _____

   _____

3. What impact do my gifts and talents make on other people?

   _____

   _____

   _____

4. How does the experience of using my talents resonate within me? Is there a desire within me to continue with this work? Do I feel a sense of fulfillment, as if the way I spend my time is in harmony with my innermost desires?

   _____

   _____

   _____

5. Do I feel stress and humiliation to a degree that I would never do this exercise again?

_____

_____

_____

6. Does the discovery of this talent give me a sense of completeness? Does it inspire me to develop my gift through more education and training?

_____

_____

_____

7. Do I look forward to the next opportunity to display my talents?

_____

_____

_____

How can identifying my talents assist me in recognizing my purpose in life

1. List some things you enjoy doing.

_____

_____

_____

2. What activities are easy for you to do?

_____

_____

_____

3. How do you feel when you engage your talents in performing these activities and/or work?

_____

_____

_____

4. Does your inner being feel relief or a great sense of satisfaction when engaging in this work/activity?

_____

_____

_____

5. Do opportunities abound, as if out of nowhere, to enable you to use your gifts and talents?

_____

_____

_____

6. Does creativity burst anew when you use your gifts?

_____

_____

_____

7. Do you derive a sense of satisfaction when you employ your talents? Do you experience a feeling of self-worth?

_____

_____

_____

8. Do you feel that you have made a great contribution to society?

_____

_____

_____

9. Do you feel a spiritual nudging that helps you understand this is your purpose in life?

_____

_____

_____

10. Is there a yearning from within that motivates you to engage your talents or gifts in a particular line of work?

_____

_____

_____

IDENTIFY YOUR MISSION.

What is MY MISSION?
(My Life's Work)

1. What areas in life do you feel passionate about?

   _____

   _____

   _____

   _____

2. When you engage in certain activities or types of work, do you feel an exuberance in knowing you have helped someone or made a difference in uplifting humanity?

   _____

   _____

   _____

   _____

3. Do you feel drawn to this work or activity?

   _____

   _____

   _____

   _____

4. When you engage in this work, do you experience a feeling of peace?

_____

_____

_____

_____

5. What activities and work do I dislike and feel most uncomfortable doing?

_____

_____

_____

_____

6. Describe your passion for your mission. What would you like to do?

_____

_____

_____

_____

_____

_____

_____

Recognizing MY ASSIGNMENT

Embracing My ASSIGNMENT in Life

1. Do a career assessment. What career fields resonate with your gifts and talents?

    _____

    _____

    _____

2. Does this career field match up with your gifts and talents? Do not forget the "passion" factor.

    _____

    _____

    _____

3. Do you feel a sense of completeness or fulfillment in this work?

    _____

    _____

    _____

4. What is the match between your gifts and your work?

    _____

    _____

    _____

5. If there is a match, you may have found your mission in life! What do you think? Write a paragraph on this marriage of your gifts to your mission.

_____

_____

_____

_____

_____

_____

_____

_____

_____

_____

_____

_____

Career Preparation

Time for Homework and Career Preparation

Now that you have begun your lifelong assessment to identify your purpose in life and you have completed the previous surveys, you are now equipped to prepare for your assignment. Think about the biography of Thaddeus Stevens and note how he began his career preparation for his assignment. He pursued a career in law. He had to relocate to a different state. His concern was not with his geographical location but with spiritual fulfillment. He wanted to make a difference in uplifting humanity. He chose the legal profession as the venue in which he would make this difference. He was concerned about the poor, uneducated, and downtrodden of society. His choice resonated with his spirit, for he, too, had known hardships and challenges in his life. His passion drove him to pursue a career in law no matter how many obstacles were placed on his pathway. When he received his degree, he worked in Pennsylvania to ensure the rights of all children, rich or poor, black or white, to receive a free public education.

As one travels the road of life, the pathways may sometimes take the traveler on unexpected turns, but the end product is the same. For Stevens, the pathway diverged when it met many smaller roads, and he found himself elected to the US House of Representatives in 1849. There, he began a long fight to rid the nation of slavery. In 1865, the Thirteenth Amendment abolished slavery in America. The battles for freedom, justice, and equality never ended for Congressman Stevens; he pursued his mission until his death. Before his death, he left directions for how his epitaph should read.

I repose in this quiet and secluded spot
Not from any natural preferences for solitude
But, finding other Cemeteries limited as to Race
By Charter Rules

I have chosen this that I might illustrate in my death
The Principles which I advocated through a long life:
Equality of Man before His Creator.

His purpose identified, his assignment embraced, and his mission fulfilled, Stevens was laid to rest in Shreiner's Cemetery. It allowed the burial of people of all races.

As Abraham Lincoln said in the Gettysburg Address, it is for us, the living, to take serious charge of our lives so that each of us may come to know his or her purpose, mission, and assignment.

Why are you important? No one's birth is an accident!
You have what it takes to be what the Creator wants you to be!

You have received an assignment from the Creator to fulfill while you are upon this earth. You can get assistance in recognizing and completing this assignment.

1. What preparation can you make to pursue your career assignment?

_____

_____

_____

_____

2. What individual(s) might assist you in your career assignment?

_____

_____

_____

_____

3. List career avenues that may be available to you.

    _____

    _____

    _____

    _____

4. What is your spiritual source and how are you using it? Do you spend time with the Creator to ask for guidance and direction?

    _____

    _____

    _____

    _____

5. Review the biography of James V. Bennett. After completing a tour in World War I, he searched for employment in the Washington, DC area. He had enrolled in law school at Georgetown University. He was offered employment in the prisons, but after a tour, he almost changed his mind because of the horrible scenes he witnessed. He murmured to his wife, "Why do I have to be my brother's keeper?" She replied with a question of her own: "Why not be your brother's keeper?" Bennett took the assignment and fulfilled his mission from 1919 until his retirement in 1964, making an impact on society by rehabilitating the US prison system. Write a paragraph on what you believe to be your career assignment to fulfill your mission between life and death.

    _____

    _____

    _____

    _____

PROTECT YOUR GIFTS AND TALENTS

Beware of Exploitation in the Twenty-First Century

There are more than 7.6 billion people on planet earth, and no one is made the same. Every person is a unique creation by God. The Creator has molded and shaped you to be a unique human being. You are the only one with your fingerprint. As we contemplate the huge variety of people in our world, we can imagine how the same Creator has individualized life assignments from person to person. You are a special individual with precious gifts given to you at birth to fulfill your mission within a specified time.

Identify and protect your gifts and talents. Do not devalue your gifts. Embrace them as a golden treasure you have received from the Creator. Living in the twenty-first century, one is confronted with many challenges regarding the exploitation of gifts. To understand the value of a gift, we need to acknowledge the gift giver. When one understands who the gift has come from, he or she must then place a high value on the gift and take very seriously the purpose for which the gift was given. Great questions to ask are these: "What is this gift?" "Why was I given this gift?" "How am I to use this gift?" "Who could benefit from my use of this gift?"

Let us look at an imaginary situation to learn more about the purpose of a gift. Let us use as an example an athlete endowed with extraordinary strength and ability to fulfill a specific purpose. Let us say he has spent time as a top teacher, educating children about caring for their bodies. But others have recognized his talents, and our athlete has been lured away from his career in teaching to play professional ball. Soon he is enjoying lucrative contracts. He has traded the more common life of a teacher for wealth, prestige, and fame. His lifestyle has taken him to the highest rung of the social ladder. Now, let us do a spiritual checklist. Who gave the athlete his ability? Before he made the change in his career, did the athlete consult with the Creator who gave the gift? Did the athlete seek to understand why he was given the gift? This individual's life has changed in terms of wealth, fame, and lifestyle. The team owners and managers are making billions from this athlete's work. How many times do we witness the deterioration of health, abuse of wealth, and shortened lives in this type of situation? As great as Mohammed Ali (Cassius Clay) was, his years of boxing took a toll on his life.

How does one protect the gifts received from the Creator? In assessing your own gifts, remember the Creator is not only the gift giver but is also the judge when the shutters close at the end of the day, the earthly lights grow dim, and life's assessment books do not balance. Can you make the best use of your gifts despite the folly of the world? Will you be true to man or true to the Creator?

HOW TO FORMULATE YOUR PHILOSOPHY OF LIFE

MY PHILOSOPHY OF LIFE

A philosophy of life is a set of goals, a plan, principles, and a set of values to serve as your guidepost as you travel your journey in life.

1. What is your philosophy of life?

    _____

    _____

    _____

2. Describe your personality. (Are you a leader or a follower?)

    _____

    _____

    _____

3. Do you have a set of rules [inside you] to guide you on life's journey? Explain.

    _____

    _____

    _____

4. Describe your value system. What are your "do's and don'ts"?

    _____

    _____

    _____

5. Do you know when to be with peers and when to be an individual? Explain.

_____

_____

_____

6. How do you plan to use your gifts and talents in life?

_____

_____

_____

7. What is most important to you—being able to earn the largest income to enhance your profile or to make a decent income and be able to give back to uplift humanity?

_____

_____

_____

8. Have you identified your purpose in life? What steps will you take to make this a reality?

_____

_____

_____

9. Are you a positive role model or mentor for your younger siblings and other youth in your community? Give two examples.

_____

_____

My Biography

(Time to Brainstorm)

1. Family Information

    _____

    _____

    _____

2. Civic and Community Work and Participation

    _____

    _____

    _____

3. Summarize your talents and tell how you use them.

    _____

    _____

    _____

4. What are your interests and aspirations?

    _____

    _____

    _____

5. Who are your models/mentors? (These are individuals who have been a positive influence in your life.)

_____

_____

_____

6. Describe what makes you happy.

_____

_____

_____

7. How do you cope with disappointment?

_____

_____

_____

8. List your honors, awards, and honorable mentions.

_____

_____

_____

9. What are your hobbies?

_____

_____

_____

10. How do you use your leisure time?

_____

_____

_____

11. Describe your best vacation.

_____

_____

_____

Setting Goals and Reaching High

(Taking the Necessary Steps to Achieve Your Goal)

1. Write a definition for *goal*.

   _____

   _____

   _____

   _____

2. Describe what it means to take the necessary steps to reach a goal.

   _____

   _____

   _____

   _____

   _____

3. List your short-range goals. (What you are planning to complete in one or two years?)

   _____

   _____

   _____

4. What steps will you take to accomplish your short-range goals?

   _____

   _____

   _____

   _____

5. What are your long-range goals? (What you are planning to do in the next three to five years?)

_____

_____

_____

_____

6. What steps will you take to achieve your long-range goals?

_____

_____

_____

_____

MY CAREER PREPARATION

1. My career interests

    _____

    _____

    _____

    _____

    _____

2. My talents, skills, and gifts

    _____

    _____

    _____

    _____

    _____

3. How do my talents complement my career interest?

    _____

    _____

    _____

    _____

    _____

    _____

    _____

    _____

4. Biographies and other books I have read

Author   *Title*   *Date Completed*

_____

_____

_____

_____

_____

_____

_____

_____

_____

_____

_____

_____

_____

_____

_____

_____

_____

_____

_____

_____

_____

_____

Worthy Home Membership

(Keep the home fires burning with love)

1. What are your tasks and responsibilities in your home?

   _____
   _____
   _____

2. Do you take pride in building your community? How do you contribute to making a positive difference on your block?

   _____
   _____
   _____

3. Do you plan your wardrobe and make preparation for the next day? What do you do the night before?

   _____
   _____
   _____

4. How is your time management? Describe how you use your time to be successful in accomplishing your goals.

   _____
   _____
   _____

5. How do you share with your family? Do you engage in a family hour, a dinner hour, and/or a prayer hour?

    _____

    _____

    _____

6. Do you reserve a quiet time on a daily basis for yourself?

    _____

    _____

    _____

7. Do you maintain a journal of daily events?

    _____

    _____

    _____

8. Do you read the Bible, poetry, and other literature?

    _____

    _____

    _____

9. What is the name of the best book you have read? Write a brief summary.

    _____

    _____

    _____

Volunteer Services: Résumé Builder

1. Do you participate in community service? Describe some of your
    activities.

    _____

    _____

    _____

    _____

    _____

    _____

2. What extracurricular activities are you affiliated with in your church,
    school, and community?

    _____

    _____

    _____

    _____

    _____

    _____

3. Do you engage in part-time work? Explain.

    _____

    _____

    _____

    _____

    _____

    _____

Reading Habits

4. How many books do you read each month? Summarize your favorite recent book.

_____

_____

_____

5. Do you read the newspaper, online news sites, or other periodicals on a daily basis? List three places you get news. Summarize one article you have recently read.

_____

_____

_____

_____

Money and Use of Money

6. Do you have a savings account or financial plan? Are you disciplined in financial matters? Are you in debt? Why? What are your plans to pay off this debt? Do you know your credit score?

_____

_____

_____

_____

MY COMMUNITY ANALYSIS

Do a survey of your community. Look around your neighborhood to answer the questions below.

1. Describe your community.

_____

_____

_____

_____

_____

_____

2. What do you like about your neighborhood?

_____

_____

_____

_____

_____

_____

3. What would you want to improve about your community?

_____

_____

_____

_____

_____

_____

4. What services or businesses would you like to have in your community? How would these services make a positive difference?

_____

_____

_____

_____

_____

_____

5. Do businesses give back to strengthen the moral fiber of your community? Do they give jobs, scholarships to youth, and maintain a clean and healthy neighborhood?

_____

_____

_____

_____

_____

_____

I Am Somebody

Cultivating My Life With Hope
Dr. Dorothy Swygert

To all people living in this world: I have a message for you. Here is a world report from me to you. I would like all people in this world to know I am an upbeat person. I have a positive personality. I do not believe anyone can keep me down if I want to be up. I want all readers out there to know I am a person of quality. If you do not understand what I am saying here and why, keep your eyes on this page and you will understand. You see, I look into the mirror daily and compliment myself. Do not get me wrong. This is not a sign that I am narcissistic or hung up on myself. It is just normal behavior. *Think about it! If you plan to succeed in this life on this planet, you must feel good about yourself.* Do not take away from the Creator and His plan. Give thanks for the blessing of your life. Remember, you must do your part in strengthening your heart so you can realize the greatness of your being.

The first thing you need to do is to give yourself a good start by kissing the dawning of the day. Make good use of your image when you get up. Look into the mirror and compliment yourself. This is not a narcissistic act; this is simply motivation. You are encouraging yourself to be a survivor on your day's journey. In order to succeed, you must know three things about yourself. *Firstly, you must know you are somebody going somewhere in life to make a positive difference.* And if you know you are important, act and carry yourself accordingly. When you hold yourself in high regard, you do not sadden your Creator by going into the world looking at others and wishing you looked like them. You look into your mirror and appreciate what you see. You smile with thanksgiving and appreciate the gifts you have been given to travel this human pathway.

Secondly, you must know you are going somewhere in life because you have been blessed with gifts, skills, and talents. You may not have the same talents as others whom you meet as you travel life's journey, but you do have your own gift package which, when properly used, can provide you with the means to not only survive but to help others in life. Help may be given in different ways, through laboring hands and spoken words as well as other ways of lifting up those around you. You may be a creative artist or an inventor. *Whatever your talents, your responsibility is to identify and develop them in a positive way to help yourself and others.*

Thirdly, you must make a positive difference as you make this journey along the human pathway. **You do not know how much time the Creator has allotted for your life. Consequently, you must view your journey with a serious heart so you can use each day to the fullest in developing and using your talents.** You do not have time to be a procrastinator, always putting things off for tomorrow. You must perceive every day as an opportunity to be the great person God created. Use your human package wisely and be sure to share the wealth. You must count each day as a blessing. When you look at others, you should wear a smile on your face and give words of encouragement.

As you give to others, you must not lose sight of your own goals and the steps and stages you must pursue in order to fulfill them. You must respect differences in the hope that others, too, will respect you. But if they do not, you still have the responsibility of fulfilling the purpose the Creator has entrusted to you. By doing this, **you can become the greatest person you are capable of being. You can make a positive difference in building a better world.** Remember, you must stay focused on the prize!

Your Response

1. How would you describe the person in this article? What does it mean to be an upbeat person?

   _____

   _____

   _____

   _____

2. According to the writer, what is the first thing one should do in the morning? Why does the writer think this act is important?

   _____

   _____

   _____

   _____

3. Describe three things the writer says everyone should do.

   _____

   _____

   _____

4. What is the meaning of *narcissism?*

   _____

   _____

   _____

   _____

5. Describe the "human package" one receives for his or her journey in life.

   _____

   _____

   _____

   _____

6. Have you ever wished you were someone else or looked like someone else? Give an example.

   _____

   _____

   _____

   _____

7. How are you using your human package?

   _____

   _____

   _____

   _____

8. How does the writer feel about procrastination? Is this a good character trait?

   _____

   _____

   _____

   _____

9. According to the writer, the Creator plays an important role in preparing one for life's journey. Explain. Give examples.

    _____

    _____

    _____

    _____

10. How can human beings help each other to succeed in life? What is *camaraderie?*

    _____

    _____

    _____

    _____

Principles

To Use in Your Journey in Life

The journey in the twenty-first century is not as easy as a trip down that magical road in *The Wizard of Oz*. It can be very challenging to "ease on down the road." As you travel down your pathway, you can look from left to right and see the vices of life dressed in colorful packages to deter you from your destination. The neon signs flash brightly in red, orange, and green, sparkling with tempting invitations. They might tempt you to make your fortune in drugs, prostitution, child trafficking, or child pornography. They might tempt you to frequent the casinos in an attempt to pay your way through college, and the list goes on. The big question is, are you focused? Are you holding tightly to your philosophy of life to guide you and enable you to fulfill your mission in life? I offer you Motivation for Your Life as you "*ease on down the road*."

Motivation for Your Life

Pretend you are packing your suitcase to take a journey. What must you take? If you want to succeed, you will need to bundle these principles on your great journey in life. Remember to take your gifts and talents and use these principles as your protection shield!

Self-Development Principles
1) Purpose
2) Respect
3) Responsibility
4) Determination
5) Discipline
6) Sacrifice
7) Faith and Fear of God

1. **Purpose:** If you know your purpose in life, you are focused! Do an assessment of your talents to help you understand your purpose in life.

2. **Respect:** If you value quality in life, you have respect for yourself and others as well as a love for humanity.

3. **Responsibility:** Identify your duties, tasks, and assignments and execute them in a timely manner. Contemplate your role as a thread in the fabric of humanity. Be accountable for your behavior.

4. **Determination:** This is your power of "stick-to-it-ness"—persistence, tenacity, a refusal to give up. With determination, you will be bound for success.

5. **Discipline:** You will need good behavioral practices to guide you in achieving your goals. Make time to be alone and time to be with others. Stay the course—no matter what!

6. **Sacrifice:** What does it mean to "have your cake and eat it too?" What does it mean to do without for a certain amount of time until you have accomplished your goals?

7. **Faith and Fear of God:** What does it mean to fear God? Why should one fear God? To fear God means to make one's behavior conform to a moral code of living. "The beginning of knowledge is to fear God" (Proverbs 1:7).

Transferrable Skills are Important

As a high school guidance counselor, I found myself reinforcing transferrable skills. "Remember," I would say to students, "you will be assuming the role of an adult in four years. Are you going to be ready?"

High school is an exciting life for an adolescent. Sometimes these students take many things for granted without assessing their skills. The three transferrable skills I emphasized to my students were *good attendance, punctuality,* and strong *interpersonal skills* in building and maintaining business and social relationships. These skills are transferrable to the world of work. The employer is seeking employees with good basic skills. Are you striving to achieve perfect attendance? Does punctuality rank high on your priority scale? Do you know how to develop good interpersonal relationships? That is, do you know how to relate to people with dignity, respect, and a sense of camaraderie?

How is your personal rating card? Do you have good manners? Have you internalized the importance of being responsible and well disciplined?

My Personal Assessment

Tasks/Traits	Good	Fair	Poor
Discipline			
Responsibility			
Goal Oriented			
Motivated in Tasks			
Good manners			
Concern for Humanity			

Parents, Prepare Your Child to Perform in the Twenty-First Century.

How to Succeed in a Knowledge-Based Global Economy

Prepare your child to succeed.

Equip your child with strong home values.

  Discipline

  Purpose in life

  Responsibility

  Respect

Encourage them to develop their gifts, skills, and talents.

Help them cultivate survival skills in a global economy.

Nurture your child to become goals-oriented.

Develop close relationships within the community at your child's school.

Parents and guardians, you can make a difference.

- Home strategies
  - Homework Check
  - School Preparation
  - Encouraging Them to Be Goal Oriented
  - Keeping a Focus on Graduation
- Good Practices at School
  - Behavior
  - Homework
  - Punctuality
  - Strong Attendance
  - Good Human Relations
- Nurturing Their Community
  - Civic Responsibilities
  - Their Role as a Model for Younger Siblings
- Camaraderie and Love of Building Humanity

STUDENTS!

- Be the best person you can be.
- Manage your time wisely.
  - Read books. Use the computer to further prepare for your career.
  - Spend quality time cultivating and developing your talents on a daily basis.
- Be courteous and polite to all people.
- Remember to use good manners: "Excuse me." "Sorry." "Forgive me." Say, "Thank you" for a kind deed.
- Keep your voice low and speak in a conversational tone as you ride the bus or train and take other public transportation. Remember to give your seat to the elderly and the infirm.
- Abstain from using profanity. Know that you are somebody of value and are above that kind of language.
- Prepare for school the night before
- Do your homework after school before you get involved with anything else
- Look into the mirror every day and say, "I am an important person, and I am going to school to develop my gifts and talents to help myself and others in a positive way."
- Tell yourself, "God gave me this breath of life, and I will not abuse it."
- Remind yourself that your purpose in life is to become the best person you are capable of becoming.
- Place value on living a life of quality. You cannot give the breath of life to another person, and you should not engage in violence and criminal activities that would take away a person's life.
- Strive to embrace humanity.
- Cultivate camaraderie. Encourage your schoolmates to do their best work, and when the opportunity arises, share your gifts to

help others. If we help each other to succeed, we can build a strong generation to build a better America as well as a just and healthy world.

- As a thread in the fabric of the America that is represented by our flag, do your part to make the country a strong nation that will lead the way in uplifting humanity.
- Be a positive role model for your brothers and sisters, relatives, and friends.

"If we fail to nurture our children today, will America exist tomorrow? Building America, block by block, one day at a time."

Dorothy Swygert

The Author's Salute to the Children of the World

Believe in Yourself
Dorothy R. Swygert

When you believe that you can
And others believe that you can't
Just believe in yourself and do the best that you can do
In striving to unfold the future for you.
Your task in life, your purpose to fulfill,
Your dreams to be accomplished
With a determined will.

BELIEVE IN YOURSELF!

Take the Pledge
A Pledge Of A Full-Fledged Human Being

I, _____

PLEDGE to direct my attention to developing my abilities and talents by striving to do my best work in school and attending and arriving for all my classes on time. I will not be satisfied with a grade of 70 when I can do better. I will raise my LEVEL OF CONSCIOUSNESS to recognize and respect the importance of living a LIFE OF QUALITY. I will remind myself every day that I AM SOMEBODY and I can make a positive contribution in this life by helping myself and others. I will engage my mind and use my leisure time in positive activities. I will spend my leisure time nurturing and developing my talents so that I may BECOME THE BEST PERSON I am capable of becoming.

Yes, I will remember I am a role model for my younger brothers and sisters, friends, and kin. Therefore, I will be conscious of BEING THE BEST PERSON I CAN BE so I can, BEGINNING TODAY, work to MAKE A BETTER TOMORROW!

As you take your journey in life, I offer you this Lantern

The Lantern

(Faith in God. Keep telling the story of hope. Nurture a spirit of love)

Teach the children by God's law, and God will bless you and your children. See Deuteronomy 11:26-28. Never mind the world; embrace God's law. Memorize and live by His law.

The Ten Commandments

1. Thou shalt have no other gods before me
2. Thou shalt not make unto thee any graven image.
3. Thou shalt not take the name of the LORD thy GOD in vain.
4. Remember the Sabbath day, to keep it holy.
5. Honor thy father and thy mother that thy days may be longer upon the land which the Lord Thy God giveth thee.
6. Thou shalt not kill.
7. Thou shalt not commit adultery.
8. Thou shalt not steal.
9. Thou shalt not bear false witness against thy neighbor.
10. Thou shalt not covet.

Strengthen the family by coming together with a
once-a-week prayer hour in your home.

You will never walk alone when you mem-
orize *The Twenty-Third Psalm.*

The Lord is My Shepherd

The Lord is my shepherd; I shall not want. He maketh me to lie down in green pastures; He leadeth me beside the still waters. He restoreth my soul; He leadeth me in the paths of righteousness for His name's sake. Yea, though I walk through the valley of the shadow of death, I will fear no evil, for Thou art with me; Thy rod and Thy staff they comfort me. Thou preparest a table before me in the presence of mine enemies: Thou anointest my head with oil; my cup runneth over. Surely goodness and mercy shall follow me all the days of my life; and I will dwell in the house of the Lord forever. (King James version)

Begin your day and end your day with:

The Lord's Prayer

Our Father who art in heaven, Hallowed be thy name. Thy kingdom come. Thy will be done on earth as it is in heaven. Give us this day our daily bread. And forgive us our debts, as we forgive our debtors. And lead us not into temptation, but deliver us from evil, for thine is the kingdom, the power and the glory, forever. **Amen**. Matthew 6:9-13.

Bring love and unity back into the family. Remember how your grandmother and great grandparents grouped the family members around the **dinner table.** No one ate until the food was blessed. This table was the nexus of love, sharing, caring, and forgiving. God is calling us once again to bring the family back unto His fold so that He can bless us and lead us according to His manual. He made us. Surely His manual is the supreme guide for living. Now, may the Lord, watch between me and thee while we are absent one from another. Spread love in your community and see the flow of God's blessings!

DARE TO BE DIFFERENT

Dorothy R. Swygert

There is more to life than exploiting your body
     by becoming a premature mother, an unequipped father.

There is more to life than being
     an inmate behind a prison wall
     where the dew drops of life never
     rise to embrace that
     magnificent person God
     meant you to be.

There is more to life than having the sharpest tongue
     rolling vulgar and profane language off your lips
     that God made to be a great orator, singer or speaker.

There is more to life than being a conformist
     ridiculing the "nerd" or
     the "goody, goody" child.

Dare to be different—to be Great in unison—in oneness

With God,. . . Our Creator.